THE SACRED SHRAVANA-BELAGOLA

(A Socio-Religious study)

THE SACRED SHRAVANA-BELAGOLA

(A Socio-Religious study)

by

Dr. Vilas Adinath Sangave

Bharatiya Jnanpith

Moortidevi Granthmala : English Granthanak 08

ISBN 978-93-263-5559-9

Printed by : Chaar Dishayen Printers, Noida

Cover : Chandra Kant Sharma

THE SACRED SHRAVANABELAGOLA
(A Socio-Religious study)
Dr. Vilas Adinath Sangave

Published by
Bharatiya Jnanpith
18, Institutional Area, Lodi Road, New Delhi-110 003
Ph. : 011-24698417, 24626467; 23241619 (Daryaganj)
Mob. : 9350536020; e-mail : bjnanpith@gmail.com
sales@jnanpith.net; website : www.jnanpith.net

Second Edition : 2017
Price : Rs. 150

DEDICATED TO

SIDDHĀNTA-CHAKRAVARTĪ ELĀCHĀRYA
MUNIŚRĪ VIDYĀNANDA-JĪ MAHĀRĀJA
FOR HIS DISTINCTIVE SERVICES AS A
GUARDIAN SAINT
OF THE ANCIENT SACRED COMPLEX OF
ŚRAVAṆA-BEḶAGOḶA

FOREWORD

It is the privilege of Bharatiya Jnanapith to publish on the occasion of the One Thousandth Year Celebrations of the installation of Gommaṭeśvar Bāhubali's Statue and its Mahamastakabhiśek at Śravaṇa-Beḷagoḷa, Karnataka, on 22nd February 1981. This remarkable book 'The Sacred Śravaṇa-Beḷagoḷa—A Socio-Religious Study' is the only book of its kind in English giving in a succinct manner an account of the environment, the shrines, the monuments and the historical development of Śravaṇa-Beḷagoḷa as also delineating the unique role of Chamundaraja in conceiving the project of getting the colossus of Bahubali carved out of a whole rock and finding sculptors who could chisel out in tangible form the intrinsic spirituality of the great Yogi that Bāhubali was. The benign smile blooming forth from the rapture of deep meditation is a living blessing that purifies the devotees and enchants the visitors.

Dr. Vilas A. Sangave is a scholar of deep study. His comprehension of his themes is always thorough, without being ponderous. Because of his rich background of history, sociology and Jain lore, he has made this study a mirror which reflects facets of Indian culture best epitomised even in the name of this pious piece of earth—Śravaṇa-Beḷagoḷa, the pond of crystal-clear waters in an idyllic setting sanctified by the meditating Shramaṇa Sādhus of yore. The utility of the book will impress, we hope, the academician as well as the general reader.

How one wishes the founders of Bharatiya Jnanpith, late Shri Sahu Shanti Prasad Jain and Shrimati Rama Jain, were sitting at the feet of Bhagwān Bāhubali on this auspicious occasion. They set the path which Bharatiya Jnanpith has been endeavouring all along to follow. Sahu Shriyans Prasad Jain as President and Shri Ashok Kumar Jain as Managing Trustee of Bharatiya Jnanpith are guiding our activities and giv ing us all encouragement to expand the activities of the Trust.

As in all such projects pursued by others on this Great Occasion, the author's source of inspiration has been Pujya Elacharya Vidyanandji Maharaj, honoured as Siddhānta Chakravartī. The blessings of His Holiness Karmayogī Bhaṭṭāraka Chārukīrtijī Swāmī of Śravaṇa-Beḷagoḷa are ever with us too.

6th February 1981

Lakshmi Chandra Jain
Director
Bharatiya Jnanpith

PREFACE

Śravaṇa-Beḷagoḷa, the most ancient and prominent sacred place of the Jainas in South India, has got a unique combination of many distinctive features which are rarely found elsewhere in the world. Throughout its long and continuous history, Śravaṇa-Beḷagoḷa has been known as a spot of scenic beauty, a place of material prosperity and a centre of spiritual and educational activities. Śravaṇa-Beḷagoḷa has also been considered as a place of great historical importance in view of the facts that it has been very closely associated from ancient times with Emperors, Monarchs, Military Generals, Prime Ministers etc., and that it has very well preserved various reliable sources of history. In fact, Śravaṇa-Beḷagoḷa has been a veritable treasure-house of all kinds of historical information of an authentic nature which is hardly found at any other single place in South India. Above all, Śravaṇa-Beḷagoḷa has got the colossal, yet contemplative, monolithic statue of Bāhubali which is regarded as one of the wonders of the world. In addition, Śravaṇa-Beḷagoḷa has been famous for its lasting contributions to the culture of the world through its classic philosophical works and exquisite sacred monuments.

In recognition of this extra-ordinary significance of Śravaṇa-Beḷagoḷa from religious, historical, architectural, sculptural, educational and other points of view, books on Śravaṇa-Beḷagoḷa have been written mainly in English, Kannada and Hindi languages. But these books are very much limited in number and were published mostly during the first half of the twentieth century. Further, these books belong to two separate categories. They are either books of a specialised nature dealing with particular aspect or aspects of Śravaṇa-Beḷagoḷa or books of a general nature giving information about Śravaṇa-Beḷagoḷa, in a cursory manner. In the circumstances a strong need was felt to have a book wrttten in English which would be not large in size but which would, at the same time, be comprehensive, authentic and academic in nature dealing with social, religious and other significant aspects of Śravaṇa-Beḷagoḷa. It is hoped that the present compendious book entitled "The Sacred Śravaṇa-Beḷagoḷa : A Socio-religious Study" will satisfy this urgent need. The book in brief, gives an account of the environment and the shrines of Śravaṇa-Beḷagoḷa; depicts the history of Śravaṇa-Beḷagoḷa from the association of Saint Bhadrabāhu and Emperor Chandragupta in the 3rd century B.C. to the present day; delineates the role of Chāmuṇḍa-Rāja, Gaṅga-Rāja and other ministers in the development of Śravaṇa-Beḷagoḷa; discusses the installation, consecration and complexion of the Bāhubali colossus at Śravaṇa-Beḷagoḷa; describes the spread of the practice of erecting on hill tops colossal and open-to-the-sky images of Bāhubali started at Śravaṇa-Beḷagoḷa; portrays the 'Mahāmastakābhisheka', i.e., the 'Grand Head Anointing' ceremonies of Gommaṭeśvara Image held at Śravaṇa-Beḷagoḷa upto the 1981 festival; presents the material and spiritual achievements of Śravaṇa-Beḷagoḷa; and analyses the contributions of Śravaṇa-Beḷagoḷa to world culture. The book also contains the specially prepared map of Karnataka State showing Jaina sacred places and the lay-out maps of Chandragiri hill, Vindhyagiri hill and village Śravaṇa-Beḷagoḷa. It is, therefore, hoped that the book will be useful to the academicians, the general readers and the tourists.

I deem it as a moral and sacred duty to mention that His Holiness Elāchārya Munishri Vindyānanda Mahārāja, who has been incessantly guiding the all-round development of Śravaṇa-Beḷagoḷa, inspired me and gave constant encouragement to me to write this book. I am highly obliged to His Holiness for this confidence shown in me.

I am really glad that this book is being published by the Bhāratīya Jñānapīṭha, the pre-eminent academic institute of India. I am further happy that this book is published on the occasion of the Grand Festival organised to celebrate in February 1981, the 1000th Anniversary of the Installation of the Image of Bāhubalī at Śravaṇa-Beḷagoḷa. I am, therefore, immensely grateful to the authorities of the Bhāratīya Jñānapīṭha and especially to its enlightened President Shriman Sahu Shreyans Prasad Jain for the publication of this book. I am also indebted to Shri Lakshmi Chandra Jain, Director of Bhāratīya Jñānapīṭha, and to Dr. Vimal Prakash Jain, Secretary, for their personal efforts in this work

I am grateful to my friend and colleague, Dr. Shantinath K. Desai, Professor and Head, Department of English, Shivaji University, Kolhapur for making valuable suggestions after carefully going through the manuscript.

I am greatly indebted to the well-equipped library of Rajaram College, Kolhapur. I am indeed grateful to the Principal and the Librarian of Rajaram College for giving me all facilities to use the rare collection of books and journals in the liberary. Similarly, I am indebted to the Shivaji University Library.

My thanks are also due to Sri H.M. Jagtap, the Cartographer for drawing the useful maps and to Shri A.G. Gosavi for preparing the neat typescript of the book.

I would be failing in my duty if I forget to offer my sincere thanks to my several friends and students who rendered to me timely help in one form or another.

Vilas Adinath Sangave

Department of Sociology,
Shivaji University, Kolhapur
January 26, 1981

CONTENTS

DIACRITICAL MARKS ADOPTED IN THIS BOOK

ङ्	ṅ	आ	ā
च्	ch	ई	ī
छ	chh	ऊ	ū
ञ्	ñ	ऋ	ṛ
ट्	ṭ	ए	ai
ठ्	ṭh	औ	au
ड्	ḍ	·	ṁ
ढ्	ḍh	:	ḥ
ण	ṇ		
श्	ś		
ष्	sh		
स्	s		
ह्	h		
ळ	ḷ		

CHAPTER-I

SIGNIFICANCE OF ŚRAVAṆA BEḶAGOḶA

1. DISTINCTIVE FEATURES

Śravaṇa-Beḷagoḷa is the most important '*tīrtha*', i.e., sacred place, of the Jainas in South India and at the same time it is a place of great cultural significance in South Indian History. This holy place with a continuous and glorious tradition of several centuries occupies a unique position among the innumerable sacred places of the Jainas found practically in all parts of India from very ancient times. It has got a rare combination of many distinctive features which are hardly present among similar places of religious nature in different parts of the world. Śravaṇa-Beḷagoḷa is famous in the world not only for its religious sanctity but also for its natural beauty, historical antiquity and architectural superiority.

From the point of view of religion, Śravaṇa-Beḷagoḷa is regarded as a significant sacred place and a prominent centre of spiritual activities of Jaina '*Sādhus*', i.e., ascetics in particular and of Jaina '*Śrāvakas*' i. e., lay followers in general. In fact the close association of the Jaina ascetics with this place is clearly enshrined in the very name of this place, viz., Śravaṇa-Beḷagoḷa. The prefix '*Śravaṇa*', attached to the name of the place is derived from the Sanskrit world '*Śramaṇa*' meaning a Jaina ascetic. Hence the term Śravaṇa-Beḷagoḷa signifies Beḷagoḷa of '*Śramaṇas*', i. e., Jaina ascetics. This is testified by the fact that from very ancient times many Jaina ascetics used to practice penance here for long periods and ultimately lay down their lives in accordance with the rule of *Sallekhanā*, i. e., willing submission to inevitable death, prescribed by Jaina scriptures. In view of this fact it is recorded in history that the great Jaina sage Bhadrabāhu, the last in line of '*Śrutakevalins*', i. e., Masters of Knowledge, and the eighth Master in succession to Lord Mahāvīra, migrated along with his 'Saṅgha', i.e., group, of 12,000 Jaina ascetics, to Śravaṇa-Beḷagoḷa from Magadha, i.e., Bihar in North India, in 3rd century B.C. Bhadrabahu was followed by his disciple, Emperor Chandragupta Maurya, who spent the rest of his life as a Jaina ascetic practising penance at Śravaṇa-Beḷagoḷa This prevalent atmosphere of serene religious sanctity surrounding Śravaṇa-Beḷagoḷa was greatly enhanced by the installation of the imposing statue of Bhagavāna Bāhubalī on the top of the Vindhyagiri hill of Śravaṇa-Beḷagoḷa in the year 981 A.D. by Chāmuṇḍa-Rāya, the renowned Military General and Prime Minister of Gaṅga Monarch Rāja-malla (IV). In the long history of religious practices connected with Jainism this event assumed considerable significance as it marked the beginning of the practice of erecting huge statues of Bhagawāna Bāhubalī and of constructing temples in his honour during the medieval period and this practice is continued even to the present day in different parts of the country. In this connection it is pertinent to note that the usual practice among the Jainas from the ancient times was to construct temples only in honour of one or more of the twenty-four '*Tīrthankaras*', i. e., Supreme Preceptors, who preached religion in this age to the benefit of the entire humanity. A New addition was made to this practice by setting at Śravaṇa-Beḷagoḷa and image of Bhagawāna Bāhubalī who was not a Tīrthankara. Naturally, it greatly increased the religious importance of Śravaṇa-Beḷagoḷa in the minds of the Jainas. Further, Śravaṇa-Beḷagoḷa has got a distinction in having a '*Māṭha*', i.e., monastery, from the early medieval period. The *Bhaṭṭārrkas*, i.e., the religious heads of the Maṭhas, wielded great power and guided the social and religious life for the Jainas in Karnāṭaka and adjacent areas. This institution of Bhaṭṭārakas is still in full swing at Śravaṇa-Beḷagoḷa. Moreover, Śravaṇa-Beḷagoḷa has got a number of old religious structures like temples, caves, pillars, etc., '*Grantha-Bhaṇḍāras*', i. e., treasures of religious scriptures and old manuscripts on different subjects and '*Pāṭhaśālas*', i. e. schools for religious instruction,

Śravaṇa-Beḷagoḷa is well-known for its scenic beauty as well as for its religious sanctity. The two hills, the tank in between, and the entire surroundings of Śravaṇa-Beḷagoḷa are so enchanting and pleasing that they invariably attract the attention of all kinds of persons. The travellers, both Indian and foreign, are highly impressed by the lively environment, green scenery and natural charm of the place. In view of this encouraging impact of nature throughout the year, the place was considered as ideal by the poets and authors for composing their creative works, by the philosophers for contemplation and by the saints for practising penance.

The sacred place of Śravaṇa-Beḷagoḷa was also famous from the point of view of the history of the region, in the sense that it was closely associated from ancient times with Emperors, Monarchs and their Generals and Prime Ministers and that it very well preserved the detailed and varied information of great historical value. In the ancient period Chandragupta Maurya, the first Emperor of India and the founder of the Mauryan Dynasty, came to Śravaṇa-Beḷagoḷa after abdicating his throne and spent the last twelve years of his life at Śravaṇa-Beḷagoḷa as a Jaina ascetic. It is believed that his grand-son Ashoka, The Great, visited Śravaṇa-Beḷagoḷa to see personally the place where Chandragupta Maurya practised penance and died according to the Jaina rite of *Sallekhanā*. In the medieval period Śravaṇa-Beḷagoḷa came to importance under the Gaṅga monarchs and later on flourished under the kings of Rāshṭrakūṭa and Hoyasala Dynasties. These Rulers and especially their able Generals and Ministers like Chāmuṇḍa-Rāya, Gaṅga-Rāja and Hulla-Rāja greatly enhanced the importance of Śravaṇa-Beḷagoḷa by erecting images, constructing temples, making endowments of lands, granting patronage to poets and scholars, practising penance and preparing themselves to die by taking the vow of *Sallekhanā*. In the modern period the Mysore kings took personal interest in preserving the prestige of Śravaṇa-Beḷagoḷa, performed the '*Mahābhishekas*', i.e., the Great Anointing Ceremonies, and granted rich endowments for upkeep of and worship at Śravaṇa-Beḷagoḷa. In the post-Independence period the same generous support has been continued by the Government of Karnāṭaka.

Apart from this close connection and continuous relationship with the rulers and administrators for centuries, Śravana-Beḷagoḷa has rendered a distnict and valueable service to historical and cultural studies in the region by supplying in large number different sources of historical data It is a matter of great pride that Śravaṇa-Beḷagoḷa has been the veritable treasure-house of all kinds of historical information pertaining to their achievements in different fields of activities. The temples, caves, pillars, statues, foot-prints, Maṭha buildings and other structures of Śravaṇa-Beḷagoḷa have provided a great amount of reliable archaeological evidence which is hardly found at any other single place in South India. Similarly, Śravaṇa-Beḷagoḷa, though small in size, has supplied a great store of authentic and trustworthy information through its huge collection of epigraphic and literary evidence in the forms of inscriptions on rocks, stone statues, metal images, metal plates, etc. and in the form of rare manuscripts written on palm leaves or papers and carefully preserved in the Maṭhas and-Grantha-Bhāṇḍāras. This kind of varied and dependable inscriptional evidence in such a large quantity is available only at Śravaṇa-Beḷagoḷa in South India. Obviously, Śravaṇa-Beḷagoḷa has become an important centre of studies in South Indian History.

Above all, Śravaṇa-Beḷagoḷa is famous all over the world for its colossal statue of Gommaṭeśvara erected on the top of its Vindhyagiri hill. This tallest and most imposing image of 57 feet in height is considered as one of the wonders of the world. Both in its conception and execution of the work of sculptural art in stone on such a grand scale and at such a high altitude open to the sky, this dignified image of a Jaina Deity is without a parallel in the world. In fact, like the Taj Mahal of Agra and the rock-cut Kailāsa temple of Ellora, this colossal and at the same time very impressive and dignified image of Gommaṭeśvara at Śravaṇa-Beḷagoḷa is the contribution of India to the civilization of the world.

In this way the sacred place of Śravana-Beḷagoḷa has been a place of spiritual significance, of natural munificance, of historical importance and of sculptural magnificance.

2. PICTURESQUE LOCATION

This most distinctive and world-renowned sacred place of the Jainas lies in the South-eastern part of the state of Karnāṭaka and is situated at 160 km. by road from Bangalore, the capital of Karnāṭaka State. It is quite convenient to reach Śravaṇa-Beḷagoḷa from Bangalore and this journey by road is most pleasant and rewarding. After leaving Bangalore by the trunk road to the Western Coast through the Marjarābāda Ghāta and on approaching Chennarāyapaṭṭaṇa at a distance of about 145 km. from Bangalore, the eye of the traveller is arrested by a conspicuous hill, a few kilometres to the south, bearing on its summit what appears at first to be a column but which on drawing nearer proves to be a colossal statue of a human being. This striking and unusal object, which is visible for miles around, marks the site of one of the most interesting spots in the south of India and of one of the significant centres of culture whose traditions carry us back to the earliest authentic period of Indian history. This place is the famous Śravaṇa-Beḷagoḷa, the chief seat of the Jainas in Southern India and their very highly revered sacred place.

Geographically the Tīrtha, Śravaṇa-Beḷagoḷa, is situated in 12°51' north latitude and 76°29' east longitude, about 15 kilometres to the south of Chennarāyapaṭṭaṇa, in the Chennarāyapaṭṭaṇa Tālukā of the Hassan District of the Karnāṭak State. This place can be comfortably reached throughout the year by the well maintained metalled roads from the important centres round about like Bangalore, Mysore, Hassan and Arsikere. Śravaṇa-Beḷagoḷa is at a distance of about :

(i) 160 km. from Bangalore, the capital of Karnāṭaka State,

(ii) 100 km. from Mysore, the capital of former princely State of Mysore,

(iii) 50 km. from Hassan, the District Headquarters and the important Railway Station on the Arsikere-Mysore section of the Meter Gauge railway line of Southern Railways, and

(iv) 70 km. from Arsikere Railway Junction on the main Poona-Bangalore Section (Broad Gauge between Poona and Miraj and Meter Gauge between Miraj and Bangalore) of the South Central and Southern Railways.

All these four road routes to Śravaṇa-Beḷagoḷa go via Chennarāyapaṭṭaṇa, the Tālukā Headquarters, which it situated at a distance of about 15 km. from Śravaṇa-Beḷagoḷa.

The term Śravaṇa-Beḷagoḷa refers to (i) the village of the same name, (ii) the hill named Vindhyagiri, (iii) the hill named Chandragiri, (iv) the tanks named Kalyāṇī, and Jakki-Katte, and (v) Chennaṇṇā's pond.

(i) The village is an ancient, ordinary, poor and small place with a population of 3628 as per 1971 Census. Capt. J. S. F. Mackenzie describes this village as 'a mean collection of houses whose inhabitants gain a precarious living by working in brass and copper' (vide 'Indian Antiquary', May 1873), The village lies picturesquely between two rocky hills, one larger than the other, which stand up boldly from the plain and are covered with huge boulders.

(ii) The larger hill known as Vindhyagiri is situared towards the South of the village and is at a height of 3,347 feet from the level of the sea and at a height of about 470 feet from the plain ground below. A flight of about six hundred steps cut in the granite rock leads upto the summit of the hill, upon which stands an open court surrounded by a bettlemented corridor containing cells, each enshrining the figure of a Jina or some other deity. The corridor is again surrounded at some distance by a heavy wall, a good part of which is picturesquely formed by boulders in their natural position. In the centre of the court on the top of the hill stands the colossal image, about 57 feet high, named Gommaṭeśvara. This huge image has been carved from the natural pointed peak of the solid rock of the hill. Apart from the statue of Gommaṭeśvara there are seven other *Bastis*, i.e., Jaina temples on this Vindhyagiri hill.

(iii) The smaller hill known as Chandragiri is situated towards the north of the village and is at a height of 3,052 feet from the level of the sea and at a height of about 295 feet from the plain ground below. A portion of this hill appears to have been known as *'Tīrthagiri'* and *'Rishigiri'*. All the *Bastis*, i.e., temples on this hill with the exception of a minor shrine stand in a walled area measuring in its greatest length about 500 feet by about 225 feet where it is widest. They are all built in the Dravidian style of architecture, the oldest of them going back probably to the eighth century. Altogether the number of temples in the walled area is thirteen and their plans are mostly similar to one another.

(iv) Between the hills of Vindhyagiri and Chandragiri there are two beautiful tanks, viz., Kalyāṇī Tank and Jakki-Katte Tank, which form part of Śravaṇa-Belagoḷa village. The Kalyāṇī Tank is a well-built tank near the western side of the village and is the first structure to be seen as one enters the village by the only main road coming from the Tālukā Headquarters Chennarāyapattana on the west. The Kalyāṇī Tank is a beautiful large pond, stepped on all sides and surrounded by a wall with gates surmounted by towers. To the north of the pond is a large pillared hall on one of the pillars of which is an inscription, No. 365, stating that the pond was caused to be built by Chikka-Deva-Rājendra, the King of Mysore, who ruled from 1672 to 1704 A.D. As the king died before the completion of this renovation work, his mint-master by name Annayyā completed the entire work with the addition of towers, pillared hall, etc. during the rule of Krishṇa-Rāja-Wodeyar I (1713-1731 A.D.), the grand-son of Chikka-Deva-Rāja. In this way, the Kalyāṇī pond which had been in existence for centuries and which was in a dilapidated condition was renovated by the kings of Mysore during the early part of the eighteenth century. The second tank, viz., Jakki-Katte, is a small tank to the south of the village and near the Bhaṇḍārī Basti, the largest temple in the village.

(v) Chennannā's pond is a small pond at some distance to the south of the village. From Inscription No. 390 it is learnt that the period of the construction of the pond was about 1673 A.D. The pond is named after the philanthropist by name Chennannā who also built a grove, a '*maṇḍapa*', i.e., hall, and a temple named Chennannā-Basti on the larger, i.e., Vindhyagiri hill.

Thus the prominent hills with heavy boulders, the built-up tank with pillared hall and towers, the natural ponds with clean water, the groves of tall coconut trees, the old temples of various dimensions scattered over the entire area, the elegant pillars with inscriptions, the large Matha with its fine wall-paintings, the serene and enchanting surroundings, the exquisite statues of different deities, and above all the most imposing image of Gommateśwara in a commanding position drawing the attention of persons for miles around undoubtedly make the village Śravaṇa-Belagoḷa the most beautiful and highly attractive spot in the region. This is testified by the views of discriminating travellers who visited the spot during the last so many centuries. In this connection the British travellers, W.H. Workman and W.J. Workman, state in their book that "In the whole beautiful State of Mysore it would be hard to find a spot, where the historic and picturesque clasp hands so firmly as here". [vide *Through Town ond Jungle* (London, 1904), p. 80]. This opinion of modern foreign travellers was regarded certainly justified by the eminent historian, Dr. B.A. Saletore, who had clearly stated that "The Jainas, much more than the Hindus, had a rare conception of scenic beauty and a gift of selecting delightful spots which were suited for religious meditation as well as for furthering the cause of material existence. Śravaṇa-Beḷagoḷa was essentially one such spot." (vide 'Jaina Antiquary', Vol. V, March 1940).

3. MEANINGFUL NAMES

The names given to the village and to the hills are very meaningful, and they do convey the long, effective and continued association of the Jainas with these places.

(i) *Śravaṇa Beḷagoḷa* :

The word Śravaṇa-Beḷagoḷa is formed by joining the two words. 'Śravaṇa' and 'Beḷagoḷa' together, and it means Beḷagoḷa of the Śravaṇas. Again, the word 'Śravaṇa' is derived from the Sanskrit word, 'Śramaṇa' meaning a Jaina ascetic. It is an established fact that the village Beḷagoḷa was closely associated with Shramaṇas or Jaina ascetics since the stay of the great sage Bhadrabāhu with his 12,000 ascetic followers and of the Mauryan Emperor Chandragupta at the hill near the village in the 3rd century B.C. and that both Bhadrabāhu and Chandragupta died on the hill according to the Jaina rite of *Sallekhanā*. In view of this sanctity attached to the place, Emperor Aśoka, the grand-son of Chandragupta Maurya, visited the place to pay his respects to his departed grandfather and it is believed that Aśoka named the place as *Śravaṇa-Beḷagoḷa* to signify the intimate relationship of Shramaṇas or Jaina ascetics with Beḷagoḷa. Further, the name Śravaṇa-Beḷagoḷa bestowed on the village Beḷagoḷa also served to distinguish it from two other Beḷagoḷa villages in the same neighbourhood, viz., '*Hale-Beḷagoḷa*', i.e., Old Beḷagoḷa, and

'*Kodi Beḷagoḷa*', i.e., Beḷagoḷa by the side of water-channel.

Later on, with the installation of the image of the God (i.e. Jina) on the hill, the term '*Śravaṇa*' assumed the meaning of Jina image and was accordingly prefixed to the hills having Jina images on them. That is why we find that the villages are named '*Śravaṇa-guṭṭa*' in the Mysore Tālukā and '*Śravaṇa-ppana-guṭṭa*' in the Malvalli Tālkuā of the Mysore District as both the places are 'guṭṭa' i.e., small hills with Jina images on them. In the same strain we find that even the place Śravaṇa-Beḷagoḷa was mentioned in the inscription No. 352 of 1634 A.D. as *Devara-Beḷagoḷa*' that is, Beḷagoḷa of the God Jina.

The usual derivation of Beḷagoḷa is from the two Kannada words '*bel*' (meaning white) and '*Kola*' by euphony '*gola*' (meaning a pond) evidently in allusion to the splendid pond in the middle of the village; and this derivation derives support from the Sanskrit equivalents '*Śveta-Sarovara*', '*Dhavala-saras*' and *Dhavala-Sarovara*' (meaning white lake) used in the inscription Nos. 67 of 1129 A.D. and No. 258 of 1432 A.D. to denote the place. That is why in some Jaina inscriptions the place is termed as '*Śukla-tīrtha*', i.e., 'bright sacred place'.

Moreover, the name *Veḷgoḷa* occurs in the inscription No. 31 of about 650 A.D., and *Beḷgoḷa* in the inscription No. 35 of about 800 A.D., Other forms of the name occuring mostly in later inscriptions are *Beḷguḷa*, *Beḷuguḷa* and *Beḷaguḷa*, which have given rise to another derivation of the name Beḷagoḷa from the herb white 'gulla' (the egg plant, Solanum ferox) in allusion to a tradition which says that a pious old women completely annointed the colossal image with the milk she had brought in a 'gulla-kāyi' or gulla fruit. The old woman was hence forward known as 'Gulla-Kāyājji'. On learning this incident saint Ajitasena, the religious preceptor of Chāmuṇḍa-Rāya who installed the colossal image on the top of the Vindhya-giri hill, remarked that "As the old woman who had brought milk in a white "gulla-kāyi' obtained celebrity by immersing the god in that milk, it is appropriate that the village should be named Beḷagoḷa". Accordingly Chāmuṇḍa-Rāya named the village as *Beḷagoḷa* and had also a stone image of old woman Gullakāyājji installed in the enclosure on the Vindhyagiri hill.

In addition, the village is also designated as '*Gommaṭapura*,' the city of God Gommaṭa, i.e., Bāhubalī, whose colossal image is the most important spot in the village. In many inscriptions the word Gommaṭapura is mentioned.

Further, in some modern inscriptions the epithet '*Dakshiṇa-Kāśī*', i.e., Benaras of the South, is applied to the village Śravaṇa-Beḷagoḷa.

On the same lines the Jainas, especially from North India, frequently refer to Śravaṇa-Beḷagoḷa as '*Jaina-Badri*', i.e., the Badri, or the most holy place, of the Jainas. Furthermore, in modern Jaina literature the village Śravaṇa-Beḷagoḷa is sometimes respectfully described as '*Abhinava Podanapura*', i.e., modern Podanapura, the capital of Bāhubali during his career as a king.

(ii) *Vindhyagiri* :

Like Śravaṇa-Beḷagoḷa, the word Vindhyagiri also denotes a spiritual meaning. The word Vindhyagiri is derived from the three words '*Vim*', meaning soul, '*Dhya*' meaning doing meditation, and 'Giri' meaning hill. Thus the word '*Vindhya-giri*' denotes 'hill for the meditation of soul'. Since many Jaina saints practised penance here in the form of meditation or contemplation, the word Vindhyagiri came to be associated with the hill.

Further, Vindhyagiri is also sometimes designated as '*Indra-giri*', i.e., the hill of God Indra. There is a beautiful statue of God Indra in the pose of holding a pot for annointing Gomma-ṭeśvara. This fine statue is erected in the centre of the pillared hall facing the image of Gommaṭeśvara. It is felt that, due to this special statue of Indra, the hill might have got the name of 'Indragiri'.

Moreover, Vindhyagiri is commonly termed in the local Kannaḍa language as '*Doḍḍa-beṭṭa*', i.e., the larger hill, distinguishing it from the other smaller hill known as 'Chikka-beṭṭa'.

(iii) *Chandragiri* :

The word 'Chandragiri' i.e., the hill of Chandragupta, has a meaning of historical nature in the sense that it signifies the most important events in the life of Emperor Chandragupta Maurya—his arrival, his long stay for 12 years, his practice of penance as a Jaina ascetic and of his ultimate death according to the Jaina rite of Sallekhanā (Chandragupta Maurya, founder of the Mauryan Dynasty, in the third century B.C.)

In the old inscriptions Chandragiri is designated as '*Kaṭava-*

pragiri' or '*Kaṭavapra*' in Sanskrit and as '*Kalvappu*' or '*Kalbappu*' in Kannaḍa.

Further a portion of the hill Chandragiri, has been referred to as '*Tīrthagiri*', i.e., the sacred hill, in the inscription No. 76 and as '*Rishigiri*;, i.e., the hill of the sages, in the inscription No. 84.

Moreover, Chandragiri is commonly termed in the local Kannaḍa language as '*Chikka-beṭṭa*', i.e., the smaller hill, distinguishing it from the other larger hill known as 'Doḍḍa-beṭṭa'.

Thus the words designating the village 'Śravaṇa-Beḷagoḷa' and its hills 'Vindhyagiri' and 'Chandragiri' are very appropriate as they correctly convey the spiritual significance and historical association of the Jainas over several long centuries.

CHAPTER-II

SHRINES OF ŚRAVAṆA BEḶAGOḶA

As the Tīrtha Śravaṇa-Beḷagoḷa has been the ancient and prominent centre of spiritual activities, the hallowed centre of attraction for the Emperors, Kings, Queens, Ministers, Generals and other dignitories, the sacred centre of meditation for the Āchāryas, Sādhus and other members of the ascetic order, the encouraging centre of inspiration for literary and cultural activities, the major seat of a Bhaṭṭāraka and the most popular place of pilgrimage of the common people in South India, it has got a large number of shrines or sacred structures of different kinds specially designed and constructed on the two hills, in the village and in the neighbouring villages.

1. ON THE VINDHYAGIRI

The entire area of the Vindhyagiri hill has been divided into two parts by a heavy wall at some distance around the colossal image of Gommaṭeśvara. This long, high and solid wall was erected in 1117 A.D. by the able minister Gaṅga-Rāja with a view to protecting the image from possible injuries. The wall has thus made the area around the image into a compact enclosure.

(A) *In the enclosure :*

The religious structures in the enclosure are as follows :

(i) The colossal *image of Gommaṭeśvara* in the centre of the west of the enclosure and facing the North.

(ii) In all *43 images* in the cloisters around the image of Gommaṭeśvara. Of these images, 2 are of Yakshī Kushmāṇḍinī, 1 of Bāhubali and 40 of Tīrthaṅkaras. The distribution of these 43 images is as under :

(a) *Eastside clositers : 14* images.
1 of Kushmāṇḍinī, and
13 of Tīrthaṅkaras.

(b) *Southside cloisters : 16* images of
16 Tīrthaṅkaras.

(c) *Westside cloisters : 13* images
1 of Kushmāṇḍinī
1 of Bāhubalī (6′ high), and
11 of Tīrthaṅkaras.

(iii) *Two images of Dwārapālakas.* i.e., door-keepers, about 6 feet high, at the sides of the entrance to the enclosure.

(iv) *One Brahmadeva Pillar*, about 6 feet above the ground level enshrining a seated figure of Brahmadeva. It is situated just near the enclosure and was caused to be made by Chāmuṇḍa-Rāya.

(v) *One figure of Gullakāyajī*, about 5 feet high, facing the image of Gommaṭa and holding a 'gulla-kāyī'. This figure is situated just near the enclosure and was caused to be made by Chāmuṇḍa-Rāya.

(B) *Outside the enclosure :*

Similarly, in the vast area outside the enclosure also there are important religious structures as given below :—

(i) *Siddhara-Basti :* It is a small temple enshrining a seated figure of a Siddha, about 3 feet high. On both sides of the figure stand two fine inscribed pillars, each about 6 feet high. These pillars show elegant workmanship, especially in their tops which are in the form of a beautiful tower.

(ii) *Akhaṇḍa-Bāgalu* : It is a door-way entrance carved out of a single rock, and on both sides of the entrance there are shrines containing the figures of Bāhubalī and his brother Bharata. According toitradition this fine doorway entrance was caused to be made by Chāmuṇḍa-Rāya.

(iii) *Tyāgada Brahmadeva Pillar* : It is an elegantly carved pillar supported from above in such a way that a handkerchief can be passed under it. It was the place where gifts were distributed and hence it is popularly known as 'Chāgada Kambha, i. e., pillar of gifts. This elegant pillar was caused to be made by Chāmuṇḍa-Rāya as recorded in inscription No. 281.

(iv) *Chennaṇṇā-Basti :* It is a temple built in honour of Chandranātha Tīrthaṅkara by Shri Chennaṇṇā. A '*mānastambha*' stands in front of it. To the north-east of the Basti is a '*maṇḍapa*' or pillared hall situated between two natural ponds.

(v) *Oḍegal-Basti :* It is a temple containing the images of Ādinātha, Śāntinātha, and Nemināṭha. Due to 'Oḍegals', i. e., stone props used for strengthening the walls of the temple, it is known as Oḍegal-Basti. It is also known as '*Trirukta-Basti*' by reason of its having three cells facing different directions. It is a fine structure, though with a plain exterior. It stands on a lofty terrace with a high flight of steps leading up to it.

(vi) *Chaturviṁśati-tīrthaṇkara Basti :* It is a small temple containing the images of 24 Tīrthaṅkaras.

(vii) *Brahmadeva-Mandira :* It is a small shrine at the foot of the hill near the beginning of the ascent. The deity is called Brahma or Jaruguppe Appa. It is a flat stone daubed with vermilion. The shrine has an upper storey, evidently a later addition, which has a figure of Pārśvanātha in it.

(viii) *Siddhara-Guṇḍu :* It it a big boulder of stone, (named after 'Siddhas', i. e., liberated souls), on which are incribed several inscriptions, the top portion being sculptured with rows after rows of seated figures representing Jaina Gurus, i.e., ascetic teachers.

2. ON THE CHANDRAGIRI

The area on the Chandragiri hill can be divided into 2 sectors, viz., (A) the temple sector, and (B) the open sector.

(a) *The Temple Sector :*

In the Temple Sector there are in all 13 temples situated as follows :

(i) *West Side of the Temple Sector :* (2 Temples)

1. *Śāntinātha-Basti :* It had once its walls and ceiling adorned with paintings, of which only a few traces are now left. The image of Śāntinātha, the 16th Tīrthaṅkara, to whom the shrine is dedicated, is a standing figure, about 11 feet high. It is not known when the temple was

erected.

2. *Supārśvanātha-Basti :* It is a small temple. It enshrines a seated Figure, about 3 feet high of Supārśvanātha, the 7th Tīrthaṅkara, canopied by a seven hooded serpent. No information is available as to when and by whom this shrine was founded.

(ii) *Middle of the Temple Sector* (7 Temples)

3. *Pārśvanātha Basti :* It is a large structure of architectural merit. The image of Pārśvanātha, the 23rd Tīrthaṅkara, about 15 feet high, canopied by a seven-hooded serpent, is the tallest on the hill. The outer walls are decorated with pilasters and miniature turrets. A lofty and elegant 'Mānastambha' stands in the front. Mānastambhas are pillars which have a pavilion at the top containing four standing or seated Jina figures facing the four directions. These differ from Brahmadeva pillars which have a seated figure of Brahma at the top.

4. *Kattale Basti :* It is the largest temple on the hill. Ādinātha, the 1st Tīrthaṅkara, to whom the temple is dedicated, is a fine seated figure about 6 feet high. It is known as Kattale Basti, i.e., temple of darkness, since it has no other opening for light than the single door in the front. It also seems to be called Padmāvati-Basti, probably from the image of that goddess found in the veranda. The temple was erected by minister Gaṅga-Rāja in the year 1118 A.D. for his mother Pochavve. The front hall of the temple is said to have been renovated by about 1850 A.D. by the ladies Devirammaṇṇī and Kempammaṇṇī of the Mysore Royal family.

5. *Chandragupta Basti :* The temple is so called because, according to tradition, it was caused to be erected by the Emperor Chandragupta Maurya. It is undoubtedly one of the oldest buildings on the hill. At the front of the temple there is an ornamental doorway with perforated stone screens at the side. The doorway is beautifully executed, each architrave consisting of five fascias of elegant workmanship. The screens are pierced with square openings in ten regular rows and the interspaces, forty-five on each, are carved with minute sculptures representing scenes from the lives of the Śrutakevali Bhadrabāhu and the

Maurya Emperor Chandragupta. The outer walls are decorated with pilasters and above them with two fine friezes, one of ornamental niches and the other of the heads and trunks of lions mostly in pairs facing each other.

6. *Chandraprabha Basti :* It is also one of the oldest buildings on the hill. It is dedicated to Chandraprabha, the 8th Tīrthaṅkara. It also has got the figures of Śyāma and Jvālāmālinī, the Yaksha and Yakshī, of this Tīrthaṅkara.
7. *Chāmuṇḍarāya Basti :* This temple, one of the largest, is the most handsome on the hill both in style and decorative features. It has also an upper storey and a fine tower. The outer walls are decorated with pilasters and crowned with three fine friezes. The outer walls of the upper storey are also ornamented with three similar friezes. It is dedicated to Neminātha, the 22nd Tīrthaṅkara. Since General and Minister Chāmuṇḍa-Rāya erected this temple by about 982 A. D., the temple is called after him. The same Chāmuṇḍa-Rāya also set up the colossal image of Gommaṭeśvara on the Vindhyagiri hill. It is also known as '*Śruta-tīrtha*', i.e., the sacred place of scriptures, because the famous saint Āchārya Nemichandra, the preceptor of Chāmuṇḍa-Rāya, composed his well known philosophical treatise entiled 'Gommaṭasāra' in this temple.
8. *Śāsana Basti :* The temple is so called from the 'Śāsana'. i.e., inscription set up conspicuously at its entrance. It is dedicated to Ādinātha, the first Tīrthaṅkara. The temple was caused to be erected by the General Gaṅga-Rāja in the year 1117 A.D.
9. *Majjigaṇṇa Basti :* It is a small temple dedicated to Anantanātha, the 14th Tīrthaṅkara. It was founded by a man named Majjigaṇṇa, but there is nothing to show when it was built.

(iii) *East Side of the Temple Sector (4 Temples)*

10. *Eraḍukaṭṭe-Basti :* This temple is so called on account of the two stairs in the east and west of the approach to it It is dedicated to Ādinātha, the first Tīrthaṅkara. The temple was caused to be built by Lakshmī-Devī, wife of the General Gaṅga-Rāja in 1118 A.D.
11. *Savatigandhavāraṇā Basti :* This temple dedicated to Śānti-

nātha, the 16th Tīrthaṅkara, is so named after the epithet 'Savati-gandhavāraṇa,' i.e., a rutting elephant to co-wives, of Śāntalā-Devī, the queen of king Vishṇuvardhana. But it is usually known as Gandhavāraṇa Basti It was caused to be built by Queen Sāntalā-Devī in 1123 A.D.

12. *Terina Basti* : This temple is so called on account of 'teru', i. e.. the car-like structure standing in front of it. It is also known as Bāhubali-Basti because of the idol of Bāhubalī or Gommaṭa enshrined in it. It was built in 1117 A.D. by two royal merchants of King Vishṇu-Vardhana.
13. *Śāntīśvara Basti* : It is dedicated to Śāntiśvara or Śāntinātha. the 16th Tīrthaṅkara. The temple stands on a high terrace and has an ornamental mortar tower. It is not known when or by whon the temple was founded.

(B) *The Open Sector* :

In the open sector on the Chandragiri hill there are some objects of interest :

1. *Kuge Brahmadeva Pillar* : This is a lofty pillar with a small seated figure of Brahmadeve on the top facing east. It commemorates the death of the Gaṅga king, Mārasiṁha II, by the Jaina rite of *Sallekhanā*, in the year 974 A.D.
2. *Mahānavamī-Maṇḍapa* : It consists of two fine four-pillared 'maṇḍapas', i.e., pillared halls, side by side facing east. Both of them have inscribed pillars set up in the middle. There are likewise several other 'maṇḍapas' containing inscribed pillars of ordinary workmanship.
3. *Bharateśvara Statue* : It is a statue, about 9 feet high, facing west, representing Bharateśvara, brother of Bāhubalī or Gommaṭa and son of Ādinātha, the first Tīrthaṅkara. The image is in an unfinished condition, being complete only to the knees, from which point it rises from the face of the rock. It may have been carved out of a large upright boulder on the spot where it stands.
4. *Bhadrabāhu Cave* : This is the cave where Śrutakevalī Bhadrabāhu lived and died. His footprints engraved on a stone slab in the cave are worshipped even now. The Maurya Emperor Chandragupta, after entering the Jaina ascetic order, remained on the hill and here worshipped these foot-prints until his death. Some devotees believe

that a look at these foot-prints every morning cures a person of any illness.

5. *Chāmuṇḍa-Rāya's Rock :* An inscribed boulder near the foot of the hill is known as Chāmuṇḍa-Rāy's rock. Tradition has it that on Chāmuṇḍa-Rāya shooting an arrow from this rock in the direction of the larger hill, as he was directed to do in a dream, the image of Gommaṭa, which had been concealed by stones, bushes, etc., became instantly visible. The rock bears figures of some Jaina saints with labels below giving their names.

3. IN THE VILLAGE

As stated earlier, the village Śravaṇa-Beḷagoḷa lies picturesquely between the Vindhyagiri Hill and the Chandragiri Hill. Like these two hills, the village, though small, has got a number of shrines in addition to some important objects of interest.

1. *Bhaṇḍārī Basti :* This is the largest temple at Śravaṇa-Beḷagoḷa, measuring about 266 feet by 78 feet. The temple is dedicated to the twenty-four Tīrthaṅkars and is hence known as the 'Chaturviṁśati-Tīrthaṅkara-Basti.' The 'garbhagṛha', i. e., the inner-hall of the temple has figures of the twenty-four Tirthaṅkaras, each about 3 feet high, standing in a line on a long ornamental pedestal. There are three doorways, the midle one being well-carved with large perforated screens at the sides of each. The figure opposite the middle doorway is Vāsupūjya, the twelfth Tīrthaṅkara, with eleven figures to its right and twelve to the left. Outside the 'garbhagṛha' there are also figures of Padmāvatī, the Yakshiṇī, i. e., the female guardian deity. and of Brahma, the Yaksha, i.e., the male guardian deity, In the front of the temple there is a fine 'Mānastaṁbha', i. e. a tall elegant pillar with a pavillion at the top containing four images facing the four directions.

The temple is popularly known as 'Bhaṇḍārī-Basti', because it was erected by Hulla-Rāja, the General and the 'bhaṇḍārī', i.e., the treasurer of the king Narasiṁha I (1141-1173 A.D.) of the Hoyasala dynasty. From inscriptions Nos. 345 and 349 it is evident that the temple was built in 1159 A.D. and that the king Na rasiṁha I, gave the name of 'Bhavya-Chūḍāmaṇī' temple and granted for its upkeep the village Sovaneru. The inscription No. 345 speaks of it thus : "The General Hulla-Rāja gladly caused this excellent Jina temple to be built with all adjuncts so that people said that it was a charming ornament of Gommaṭapura. Together with its enclosure, dancing hall, two fine strongly built large Jaina dwellings at the sides, and mansion with doorways resplendent with various elegant ornaments of foliage and figures, the matchless temple of Chaturviṁśati-Tīrthaṅkaras, resembling a mass of religious merit, was thus completed by Hulla-Rāja." For constructing this remarkable Jaina temple in the central square and in front of the large Jaina Maṭha building of the village and for his pious and strict religious behaviour, the State Treasurer and General Hulla-Rāja was given the title of "Samyaktva-Chūḍāmaṇi".

2. *Akkana Basti :* This is the only temple in the village built in the Hoyasala style of architecture. On the central pedestal there is a standing figure, about 5 feet high, of Pārśvanātha, the 23rd Tīrthaṅkara, sheltered by a seven-hooded serpent. There are also fine figures of Dharaṇendra and Padmāvatī, the Yaksha and Yakshī of this Tīrthaṅkara. The hall of the temple has four beautiful black stone pillars ornamented with bead work and nine elegantly executed ceilings which are nearly two feet deep. The pillars are polished and have a shining surface like those of the famous Pārśvanātha temple at Bastihaḷḷi near Haḷebid. The tower of the temple has on its front embankment a beautiful panel very artistically carved with scroll work and surmounted by a lion's head. The panel has a seated Jina figure in the centre and the embankment has at its sides figures of Saraswatī.

From the inscripition No. 327 it is clear that the temple was erected in 1181 A.D. by the Jaina lady Achiyakkā, wife of Chandramauli, the Brahminī Minister of the Hoyasala king Ballāḷa II and that the king granted for its upkeep the village Bammeyanahaḷḷi. The temple is called Akkana Basti, which is a shortened form of Achiyakkana Basti, that is, the Basti founded by lady Achiyakkā.

3. *Siddhānta Basti :* It is situated in the west enclosure of Akkana-Basti. It is so called because all the important

books bearing on the Jaina 'Siddhānta', i.e., basic philosophy, were once secured in a dark room of this temple. It is said that at some remote period 'Dhavalā', 'Jayadhavalā' and other rare philosophical works were carried away from this temple of Mūdabidrī, the sacred place and the seat of a 'Bhaṭṭāraka', in the South Kanara District of Karnāṭaka. It appears that the great authors and saints like Āchārya Nemichandra must have taken advantage of this rare treasure of philosophical works preserved in the temple.

4. *Dānaśāle Basti :* This a small temple situated near the entrance to the Akkana-Basti. It enshrines a 'Pañcha-Parameshṭhī'image, about 3 feet high. It is recorded that Doḍḍa-Deva-Rāja-Oḍeyār (1659-1672 A.D.), the King of Mysore,made a grant of the village Madaneya for the upkeep of this temple at the instance of his prince Chikka-Deva-Rāja-Oḍeyār and during the latter's visit to Śravaṇa-Beḷagoḷa.

5. *Nagara-Jinālaya :* It is a small temple dedicated to Ādinātha, the first Tīrthaṅkara. From the inscription No. 335 in the temple it is evident that it was caused to be erected in 1195 A.D. by the minister Nāgadeva of the Hoyasala King Ballāḷa II (1173-1220 A.D.). The temple was named 'Nagara-Jinālaya', because the 'Nāgara', i.e., city merchants were its supporters. It also appears to have borne another name 'Shrī-nilaya'.

6. *Maṅgāyi Basti :* This plain temple is dedicated to Sānti-nātha, the 16th Tīrthaṅkara. In front of the temple are two well carved elephants. Inscriptions Nos. 339 and 341 state that the temple was caused to be built by Maṅgāyi of Beḷuguḷa, a disciple of Abhinava-Chārukirti-Paṇḍitāchārya and a crest jewel of royal dancing girls, and that it was named 'Tribhuvana Chūḍāmaṇī' temple. It was built in 1325 A.D. Further, the inscription No. 337 on the pedestal states that the statue was caused to be made by Bhīma-Devī, a lay disciple of Chārukīrti Paṇḍitāchārya and the queen of Deva-Rāya-Mahārāya. This Deva-Rāya was most probably the Vijayanagar King Deva-Rāya I (1406-1416 A.D.).

7. *Jaina Maṭha :* The Jaina Maṭha, which is the central

place of residance of Bhaṭṭārak Chārukīrti, is a pretty structure with an open courtyard in the middle. It was an one-storey structure and by 1910 A.D., an upper storey was added to the building The pillars of the porch are elegantly carved. The Maṭha has three cells standing in a line, facing west, which contain the metal and stone images that are daily worshipped. These images appear to have been presented by the people of Tamil Nadu during 1850 to 1858 A.D. The remarkable feature of the Maṭha is the wall paintings illustrating mostly scenes from the lives of of some Tīrthaṅkaras and the Jaina king Nāgakumara. In the Maṭha there are eight idols made out of precious stones like ruby, sapphire, coral and emerald.*

4. NEAR THE VILLAGE

In the villages adjacent to Śravaṇa Beḷagoḷa also there are a number of ancient Jaina shrines which are well-known in the region not only for their antiquity but also for their architectural beauty

1. *Śāntinātha-Basti at Jinanāthapura* : The village Jinanāthapura, situated about one mile to the north of Śravaṇa-Beḷagoḷa, was founded by Ganga-Rāja, the General of the Hoyasala king Vishṇuvardhana in about 1117 A.D.. The village is famous for its Śāntinātha-Basti, i.e., the temple dedicated to Śāntinātha, the 16th Tīrthankara. This Śāntinātha-Basti is a very fine specimen of the Hoyasala style of architecture and in fact it is regarded as the most ornate of the Jaina temples in the Karnāṭaka State. The image of Śāntinātha is a well carved figure about 5½ feet high. The hall of the temple has four elegantly executed pillars adorned with bead work and nine good ceilings, each about 1-1/2 feet deep. The outer walls of the temple are the most distinguishing features of the temple as they have a row of large images surmounted by beautiful turrets and scrolls. The images consist of Tīrthankaras, Yakshas, Yakshīs, Brahma, Saraswatī, Manmatha, Mohinī, drummers, musicians, dancers, etc.

---

* *Recently the work of extention of the Matha building was carried out in June 1980 by Constructing in Modern style a two-storeyed structure known as "Bhattaraka Bhavana.*

From the inscription No. 380 on the pedestal we learn that the temple was founded by the General Vasudhaika-bāndhava Rāchimayya, who was first the minister of the Kalachūrya king and later on placed himself under the protection of the Hoyasala king Ballāḷa II (1173-1220 A.D.). Hence the period of the erection of the Śāntinātha-Basti is put about 1200 A.D. This Basti was renovated in 1632 A.D. by Pāleda-Padumaṇṇa.

2. *Aregal-Basti at Jinanāthapura :* In the east of the village Jinanāthapura there is another temple, known as Aregal-Basti, which is older than Sāntinātha Basti. It enshrines a fine seated marble image of Pārśvanātha, the 23rd Tīrthaṅkara, about 5 feet high and canopied by an eleven-hooded serpent. The temple is very neatly kept. It is called Aregal-Basti because it is built on 'aregal', i.e., a rock.

From the inscription No. 383 on the pedestal we learn that the image was set up so recently as 1889 A.D. for the spiritual welfare of one Bhujabalaiyā, a resident of Beḷagoḷa. This was done because the original image had suffered mutilation. The original image, a standing figure, is now lying in the bed of the tank closeby.

3. *Pārśvanātha-Basti at Haḷe-Beḷgoḷa :* The village Haḷe-Beḷgoḷa is at a distance of about four miles to the north of Śravaṇa-Beḷagoḷa and is known for its ruined Jaina temple in the Hoyasala style of architecture. The temple has a mutilated standing figure of Pārśvanātha, the 23rd Tīrthaṅkara, about 5 feet high, with a seven hooded canopy and a serpent coil behind. In the hall of the temple there are beautifully carved figures of 'ashṭa-dikpālakas,' i.e., regents of the eight directions, of Yaksha Dharaṇendra with a five-hooded canopy and of chauri-bearers. The temple was built about 1094 A D.

4. *Old Basti at Sane-haḷḷi :* The village Sane-haḷḷi, about three miles from Śravana-Beḷagoḷa, has a ruined Jina temple which was caused to be built in about 1120 A.D. by Jakkimavve, the wife of the elder brother of Gaṅga-Rāja, the General of the Hoyasala king Vishṇuvardhana.

5. *Jaina Pillar and Pañchakūṭa-Basti at Kambad-haḷḷi :* The small village Kambada-haḷḷi is situated at 11 miles from Śravaṇa-Beḷagoḷa by a bullock cart track and is known for its lofty Jaina pillar near its north-west corner. In fact the name of the village is derived from the pillar as 'Kambada-haḷḷi' means

1. A bird eyeview of Chandragiri.
[A. S. I. New Delhi.]

2. Some temples on Chandragiri in their natural setting

[A.S.I. New Delhi]

3. Chamundaraya Basadi on Chandragiri.
[A. S. I. Mysore]

4. Parshvanatha Basadi and Manastambha on Chandragiri

5. A feneral view of Vindhyagiri and Kalyani Tank.

(A. S. I. Mysore)

6. Gommateshvara Bahubali

7. Tyagad Brahmadeva Pillar (in centre)

[A.S.I. New Delhi]

8. Artistic richness of the outer wall of Shantinatha Basadi at Jinanathpur.

village of the pillar. This pillar with a seated Brahma on the top is especially elegant. Similar pillars we find on the Vindhyagiri and Chandragiri hills at Śravaṇa-Beḷagoḷa. It is considered as one of the most elegant pillars in the Karnāṭaka State.

To the west of this pillar stands a group of five shrines belonging to the oldest monuments of Jainism in the Karnāṭaka State. The earliest structure with an image of Ādinātha, the first Tīrthahṅkara, in its cell may be dated about 900 A.D. according to the plan and the decorative details of very early Dravidian design. The towers above the shrines are of various shapes: round, square and octagonal. But everywhere the dome is bulbous. Further, the Tīrthaṅkara figures are found lying scattered everywhere. Moreover, there appears to have been a compound wall enclosing these five shrines thus making a complex of five temples generally known as 'Pañchakūṭa Basti'. Again, about twenty feet to the north of this compound wall is another large temple some interior chambers of which have been destroyed; the main image of Śāntinātha, the 16th Tīrthaṅkara, however, and that of a female goddess are fortunately well preserved. The high basement of this temple has a finely carved frieze of ridden horses, elephants and lions. This temple, immediately preceding the Hoyasala style of architecture, may be attributed to the beginning of the twelfth century A.D.

In view of these old Jaina relics of great architectural value it can be said that, if the communication facilities are improved, the Kambada-haḷḷi will beccome an important place of pilgrimage for the Jainas.

CHAPTER-III

EARLY HISTORY OF ŚRAVAṆA-BEḶAGOḶA

1. SOURCES OF HISTORY

As Jainism was a very powerful influence that moulded the religious and cultural life of entire South India during the early and medieval epochs of its history, it had a number of important centres, scattered over different areas of South India, These centres were virtually strongholds of the varied activities of the Jainas for several centuries. Among such significant centres in South India the sacred place of Śravaṇa-Beḷagoḷa enioyed a prominent position. This sacred complex of Śravaṇa-Beḷagoḷa not only wielded consideradle influence on the cultural life of the Jainas and others in the region but also effectively served as a direct connecting link between the Jainas of South India and the Jainas of North India from very early times. That is why Śravaṇa-Beḷagoḷa has been really fortunate in having its continuous history right from the ancient times to the present day. In tracing this uninterrupted history Śravaṇa-Beḷagoḷa is also fortunate because it possesses in an unusually large measure and in a very safe condition the following three major sources of history :

1. Inscriptions,
2. Local traditions and literature, and
3. Antiquities such as the remains of sculptures, paintings, and old structures like caves, temples, pillars, Maṭhas, tanks, etc.,

These three categories of sources are mutually corroborative and they constitute important links in the historical account of the place and the region.

As regards the source of inscriptions Śravaṇa-Beḷagoḷa has got a very distinctive position in undestsanding the history of the Jainas in South India. It is true that there are other important places in Karnāṭaka like Aihoḷe in the Bijapur District, Malakhed in the Gulbarga District and especially Koppal in the Raichur District, which are famous for their very informative and authentic Jaina inscriptions. But these inscriptions are limited in number and, though ancient, pertain to a restricted period upto the medieval ages. On the other hand the inscriptions of Śravaṇa-Baḷagoḷa are not only much numerous but they cover a much longer period stretching from the ancient times upto the last quarter of the nineteenth century. Moreover, the inscriptions of Śravaṇa-Beḷagoḷa have been more varied and valuable as Śravaṇa-Beḷagoḷa acquired great importance as a centre of cultural activities and as a place of pilgrimage with the installation of the colossal image of Gommaṭeśvara in 981 A.D.

It is estimated that there are more than five hundred inscriptions in and around the village Śravaṇa-Beḷagoḷa. These numerous ancient inscriptions engraved on rocks of the Vindhyagiri and Chandragiri Hills, on the pillars, walls, slabs and pedestals of the temples and on metal plates and images in Śravaṇa-Beḷagoḷa were unfortunately not completely known to the public as no adequate efforts were made to read and understand them. This pathetic position of the Jaina inscriptions at Śravaṇa-Beḷagoḷa was described in a note dated 19th July 1873 by Mr.B.Lewis Rice, the great archaeologist and oriental scholar, in the following words: "At the Jaina village of Śravaṇa-Beḷagoḷa, on a smaller hill named Chandra-Biṭṭa, facing the loftier Indra-Biṭṭa, on which stands the colossal image of Gommateśvara, are a number of inscriptions cut in the rock both on the summit and around the sides. The characters in which they are engraved are of a curious elongated form, measuring a foot or more in length, strikingly distinct in the rays of the sun, but scarcely distinguishable when in shade. The inscriptions consist mostly of three or four lines apiece, and are scored about in all directions, without any appearance of order. The learned men attendant on the Jaina pontiff of the neighbouring 'Maṭha' can neither read the characters, nor give any account of the inscriptions." (vide "Indian Antiquary", September 1873, pages 265-266).

With a view to change this lamentable position of the valuable inscriptions strenuous and devoted efforts were made by Mr.B.Lewis Rice, C.I.E., M.R.A.S., in his capacity as the Director of Archaeological Researches in Mysore State. As a result, Mr.B.Lewis Rice deciphered and published 144 inscriptions for the first time in the year 1889 in the book entitled, "Inscriptions at Śravaṇa-Beḷagoḷa". This pioneering work of Mr.B.Lewis Rice in the field of bringing to light the inscriptions at Śravaṇa-Beḷagoḷa was further continued in the most sucessful and able manner by Prāktana-Vimarsha-Vichakshaṇa, Rao Bahadur R.Narasiṁhāchār, M.A., M.R.A.S., the Director of Archaeological Researches in Mysore State. Eventually Shri Narasiṁhāchār succeeded in deciphering, translating and editing as many as 500 inscriptions ranging from 600 A.D. to 1889 A.D. and in publishing them in 1923 A.D. in the voluminious work entitled "Epigraphia Carnatica, Vol.II, Inscriptions at Śravaṇa-Beḷagoḷa". Obviously this monumental work of Shri Narasiṁhāchār has proved a great boon in understanding the history of Śravaṇa-Beḷagoḷa as it sufficiently revealed for the first time the rich and hidden heritage of Śravaṇa Beḷagoḷa. But this detailed historical information of great cultural value contained in the scholarly treatise of Shri Narasiṁhāchār could not reach the general public as the book was written in English and the texts of the inscriptions were given in the Roman script. With a view to obviate these difficulties Dr. Hira Lal Jain, M.A., LL.B., Ph.D., the great oriental Scholar and Jainologist, translated the treatise in Hindi and gave the texts of the inscriptions in the Devanāgarī script in his book entitled "Jaina-Śilālekha-Saṅgrahaḥ" published in 1928 A.D. Really the entire credit of unearthing the history of Śravaṇa-Beḷagoḷa must go to these devoted archaeological researchers and oriental scholars.

This treasure of 500 inscriptions was scattered at different places in the sacred complex of Śravaṇa-Beḷagoḷa as follows :

Sr. No.	*Location of Inscriptions*	*No. of inscriptions*
1.	On the Chandragiri Hill	244
2.	On the Vindhyagiri Hill	161
3.	In Śravaṇa-Beḷagoḷa village	65
4.	Near Śravaṇa-Beḷagoḷa village	30
	Total :	500

It is clear that the Chikka-Beṭṭa, i.e., the Chandragiri Hill is more important from the point of discovery of the inscriptions as practically half of the rich collection of inscriptions was found there. Further it is interesting to note that out of these 244 inscriptions on the Chandragiri Hill, a very large number of epigraphs was located especially in front of the Kattale-Basti and to the south of the Pārśvanātha-Basti on the hill. Again, these inscriptions on the Chandragiri Hill have greater historical significance as they are more ancient compared to the inscriptions found at other places in the sacred complex of Śravaṇa-Beḷagoḷa.

Moreover, these inscriptions are more varied in nature in the sense that they are written in different languages and in various scripts. The inscriptions are in Prakrit, Sanskrit, Kannaḍa, Tamiḷ and Marāṭhī languages and according to the characters in which the inscriptions are written we find that there are :

45 in Devanāgarī script,
17 in Mahājanī script,
11 in Grantha and Tamiḷ script,
1 in Vaṭṭeluṭṭu script, and
426 in Kannaḍa script,

As regads the period of these inscriptions we can note that they cover a very long range of nearly thirteen centuries as they pertain to the period from 600 A.D. to 1889 A.D., Even in this period many epigraphs belong to the period from the 7th to the 12th century A.D. and especially to the 7th and 8th centuries.

Furthermore, many of the inscriptions are of great historical importance as they supply various kinds of information useful to the historian, the archaeologist, the sociologist and the other scientists. For example, a good number of inscriptions refer to specific dynasties of kings such as the Gaṅga, the Rāshṭrakūṭa, the Chālukya, the Hoyasala and to the kings of Vijayanagar and Mysore. The epigraphs relating to the Hoyasala dynasty are fairly numerous. There are also a few records which refer to the Kadaṁbas, the Nolaṁbas, the Choḷas, the Chāṅgaḷvas, and the chiefs of Nidugal and Nuggehaḷḷi. Again in the early inscriptions we get references to various areas and places like Agare, Kottera, Veguru, Alpura, Ādiyarenāḍu, Dakshiṇa Madhurā, Kittur, Veḷgoḷa, Malanur, etc. They also mention frequently the names of Digaṁbara Jaina saints belonging to Mūla-Saṅgha, Sena-Saṅgha, Deva-Saṅgha and Nandī-Saṅgha. Similarly, they give information about religious practices and ceremonies. In general, the inscriptions are of great interest in several ways. A good number of them record the visits of kings, queens, ministers, generals, divines, scholars, poets and artists. Several of them are fine specimens of Kannaḍa and Sanskrit compositions. Many furnish items of important information bearing on history and religion.

Apart from inscriptions, the literature and local tradition also serve as source of the history of Śravaṇa-Beḷagoḷa. Many poets and saints of repute and authority have got inspiration from the sacred environment of Śravaṇa-Beḷagoḷa, especially from the colossal image of Bāhubalī. Their beautiful poetic compositions and learned religious treatises provide varied information about the place. Poets have composed verses on the beauty and grandeur of the image of Gommaṭeśvara in many languages. The names of great Kannaḍa poets like Ranna, Sujanottaṁsa, and Madhura and of great Jaina saints like Ajitasena, Āchārya Nemichandra, etc., are closely associated with Śravaṇa-Beḷagoḷa. The great General and Minister Chāmuṇḍa-Rāya, who installed the superb image of Gommaṭeśvara, was a patron of many poets. The writings of these poets and other authors do supply additional information of a reliable nature about Śravaṇa-Beḷagoḷa in different periods.

Like epigraphs and literary works, the antiquities also serve as a significant source of history of Śravaṇa-Beḷagoḷa. The sacred complex of Śravaṇa-Beḷagoḷa has been very forrunate in having a large number of antiquities like statues, structures, paintings, etc. and that too in a comparatively good condition, as such relics are not found in other ancient and prominent Jaina sacred places in Karnāṭaka, like Malakheda in Gulburga District and Koppal in the Raichur District. Many of these relics are works of art and as such they throw sufficient light on the architectural and sculptural glory of Śravaṇa-Beḷagoḷa.

Thus, with the help of numerous and reliable inscriptions, literary works and antiquities, the history of Śravaṇa-Beḷagoḷa can be traced continuously from the ancient times of saint Bhadrabāhu and Emperor Chandragupta Maurya to the present day.

2. ASSOCIATION OF BHADRABĀHU AND CHANDRAGUPTA

It was held by many writers that the history of Jainism in South India starts when the famous saint, Bhadrabāhu, the head of the Jaina ascetic order, with his 12000 followers and his disciple Emperor Chandragupta Maurya, migrated from North India, to Śravaṇa-Beḷagoḷa in South India, by the end of the third century B.C. with a view to protecting and preseving the religion in its pristine purity from the impending fear of the long protracted conditions of severe famine in North India. This view of correlating the advent of Jainism in South India with the migration of Bhadrabāhu and Chandragupta to Śravaṇa-Beḷagoḷa in the third century B.C., was maintained in historical writings for a considerable time. But recent researches in South Indian history have discredited this view and have convincingly shown that Jainism must have been in existence in South India even before the arrival of Bhadrabāhu and Chandragupta. The reasons put forward for this recent view may be briefly stated as follows :

(i) Before Bhadrabāhu made up his mind to migrate towards the South with his royal disciple and a large body of monks, he must have been confident of the favourable nature of reception he was going to have in the land of his destination. This, therefore, indicates the earlier existence of the followers of the Jaina religion in the southern parts of Karnaṭāka and Tamiḷ Nāḍu.

(ii) In the Buddhist work 'Mahāvaṁsa' (translated by wilhelm Geiger and published by Pali Text Society, London, 1912-) it is stated that Jainism was prevalent in the island of Ceylon during the 4th century B.C. The most reasonable view regarding the immigration of the Jaina faith to the island of Ceylon would be to hold that it travelled all the way from North India by land route through South India. This suggests a date anterior to the 4th century B.C., for the advent of Jainism in South India.

(iii) Tamil Nāḍu appears to have come under the influence of Jainism earlier than the infiltration of the Vedic or Brahmanical faith from North India. This is suggested by the imprint of Jaina ideas and concepts noticeable in the early Tamil works like Kural and Tolkappiyam. The origin of another early Tamil work named Naladiyāra is couched in Jaina associations. This work, as the tradition goes, is a composite writing of eight thousand Jaina monks departing from the Pāṇḍyan kingdom against the wishes of its ruler who was attached to their faith.

It is thus evident that Jainism was the prevalent faith in South India for many centuries before the Christian Era and that the region of Śravaṇa-Beḷagoḷa must have been a prominent centre of Jaina religion in South India by the 3rd century B.C. But it is also clear that the known history of Śravaṇa-Beḷagoḷa commences from its association with Bhadrabāhu and Chandragupta by the end of the 3rd century B.C.

The great Jaina saint Bhadrabāhu, who came down from the North to Śravaṇa-Beḷagoḷa with a large group of followers numbering 12,000 during the last quarter of the 3rd century B.C., was the most eminent authority in the Jain ascetic order as he was the eighth teacher or authority in succession after the passing away of Lord Mahāvīra in 527 B.C. The first three teachers or authorities, viz,, Gautama, Sudharma, and Jambūswāmī, were styled as *'Kevalins'*, i.e., the Perfect Omniscients, and the latter five teachers or authorities, viz., Nandī, Nandīmitra, Aparājita, Govardhana and Bhadrabāhu were termed as *'Śrutakevalins'*, i.e., the Omniscients not so perfect. A 'Śrutakevalī' is one who knew almost the entire Jaina scriptures in their crystalline purity and who had the power of reading the past and the future. According to Jaina scriptures, Bhadrabāhu was the last in the line of these Śruta-kevalins.

The career and work of Bhadrabāhu have been outlined in many distinguished literary works like 'Bṛhat-Kathākosha' and 'Bhadrābahu-Charitra' in Sanskrit and 'Munivaṁśā-bhy-udaya', 'Vaddārādhane', and 'Rājāvalikathe' in Kannada. According to these sources, Bhadrabāhu was born in the town Koṭikapura in Puṇḍravardhana (i.e. Pubna in Bengal) as the son of Somaśrī and Soma-śarmā who was the 'Purohita', i.e., the priest to king Padmaratha. When this boy was playing on the road one day, he was seen by Govardhana (the 4th Śruta-kevalī or the 7th teacher after Mahāvīra), who was passing that way. The venerable Śrutakevali was greatly impressed by the bearing and confidence of the boy and with the permi-ssion of the parents took him along with him. The boy grew up under the personal care of the 4th Śrutakevalin and soon distinguished himself as the master of the religious scrip-tures. As a young man Bhadrabāhu was admitted into the ascetic order and he practised severe austerities. He was not reputed as a great scholar, but venerated as a saint of high spiritual attainments. In due course, he became '*Āchārya*', i.e. the Head of the Jaina Saṅgha which at that time was undivided.

Once it so happened that Chandragupta Maurya (322-298 B.C.) who was then the Emperor of Magadha, had sixteen dreams and the sixteenth dream pertained to a twelve-hooded serpent. Bhadrabāhu, who was invited to interpret the dreams, foresaw a dreadful famine that would overtake the kingdom for a twelve year period. Bhadrabāhu feared that he and his ascetic order would find it hard to keep to their austere prac-tices during these troublesome days, and decided to migrate to the regions south of the Vindhyas. The Emperor Chandragupta Maurya, who was very much devoted to the saint, made over the empire to his son Bindusāra and joined Bhadrabāhu's entourage as a monk-disciple.

This party of ascetics, 12000 in number, led by Bhadrabāhu, left Magadha and moved Southwards. This was but one section of the Jaina community, and the other section continued to stay in Magadha under Sthūlabhadra. The disciples of Bhadrabāhu arrived in Śravaṇa-Beḷagoḷa in South India. It was then a pleasant clearance on the hill in the midst of a dense jungle called '*Kaṭavapra*'. While in Śravaṇa-Beḷagoḷa, Bhadrabāhu perceived that his end was near and he decided to stay there. He sent the party of ascetics onwards to the Choḷa and Pāṇḍya kingdoms placing his disciple Viśākhāchārya in charge of it. Chandragupta alone stayed on in Kaṭavapra serving his aged master. Bhadrabāhu spent his last days in a cave on the hill, engaged in severe penance and ultimately died by taking the vow of '*Sallekhanā*', i.e., willing submission to inevitable death. This cave, known as Bhadrabāhu Cave, became in course of time a shrine where devout monks and laymen spent their last days performing severe austerities. Bhadrabāhu is said to have lived for 76 years and died by about 297 B.C.

Chandragupta, the devout ascetic disciple of Bhadrabāhu, lived for 12 years after death of his teacher Bhadrabāhu. In this ascetic life Chandragupta practised penance on the same hill and died according to the strict Jaina rite of 'Sallekhanā', Chandragupta's death occurred when he was about 62 years of age.

This fact of direct association of Bhadrabāhu and Chandragupta with Śravaṇa-Beḷagoḷa, popularly known as 'Bhadrabāhu-Chandragupta tradition', is strongly supported by a large number of epigraphic, archaeological and literary evidences of a very reliable nature. These evidences can be briefly cited as follows :

(1) *Chandragiri Hill :* The smaller hill at Śravaṇa-Beḷagoḷa is said to derive its name Chandragiri from the fact that Chandragupta lived and performed penance there for 12 years.

(2) *Chandragupta-Basti :* The Chandragupta-Basti, one of the oldest temples on the same hill, is said to be so called because it was caused to be erected by Chandragupta. Moreover, the facade of this Basti which is in the form of a perforated screen, contains 90 sculptured scenes depicting events in the lives of Bhadrabāhu and Chandragupta.

(3) *Bhadrabāhu Cave :* There is a cave on the same hill, known as Bhadrabāhu cave, containing his footprints, in which he is said to have expired. Inscription No. 166 of about 1100 A.D. in the same cave refers to worship being done to the footprints of Bhadrabāhu for a long time,

(4) *Śrīrangattaṇ Inscriptions :* Two inscriptions on the north bank of the river Kāverī near Śrīraṅgapattaṇ, of about 900 A.D., describe the summit of Kalbappu hill or Chandragiri as marked by the impress of the feet of the great sages Bhadrabāhu and Chandragupta.

(5) *Śravaṇa-Beḷagoḷa inscriptions :*

(i) Among the inscriptions at Śravaṇa-Beḷagoḷa itself, Inscription No. 31 of about 650 A.D. refers to the pair of the great sages Bhadrabāhu and Chandragupta, and states that the Jaina religion, which had greatly prospered when they shed lustre on it, having become little weak, the sage Śāntisena renovated it.

(ii) Again, Inscription No. 67 of 1129 A.D. mentions Bhadrabāhu and Chandragupta who, through the merit of being his disciple, was served for a long time by the forest deities.

(iii) Further, Inscription No. 64 of 1163 A.D. speaks of Bhadrabāhu, the last of the Śrutakevalīs, and of his disciple Chandragupta, by whose glory the sages of his '*gaṇa*' i.e., section, were worshipped by the forest deities.

(iv) Moreover, Inscription No. 258 of 1432 A.D., after extolling the lord of ascetics Bhadrabāhu, says that his disciple was Chandragupta, who was bowed to by the chief gods on account of his perfect conduct and the fame caused by the greatness of whose severe penance spread into other worlds.

(6) *Literary Evidences :* (i) A Sanskrit work entitled '*Brihatkathākosha*' written by poet Harisheṇa in 981 A.D. says that Bhadrabāhu, the last of the Śrutakevalīs, had the king Chandragupta as his disciple. It gives a detailed account of the life of Bhadrabāhu.

(ii) Another Sanskrit work, named '*Bhadrabāhucharitra*', by Ratnanandī, which appears to belong to about the 15th century, also gives an account of Bhadrabāhu's exodus to Karnāṭaka and states that Viśākhāchārya, the disciple of Bhadrabāhu, led the Jain Saṅgha at the instance of his guru to the Choḷa country. It also refers to the penance practised and the foot-prints of Bhadrabāhu worshipped by Chandragupta Muni.

(iii) The Kannaḍa work '*Munivaṁśabhyudaya*', written in 1680 A.D. by poet Chidānandakavi, gives incidentally same information about Bhadrabāhu and Chandragupta.

(iv) Another Kannaḍa work '*Rājāvalikathe*' written by poet

Devachandra in 1838 A.D. furnishes the details regarding the migration of Bhadrabāhu and Chandragupta to Mysore region and tells us that Bhadrabāhu, at the time of his death, nominated his disciple Viśākhāchārya as the leader of the assemblage of monks and instructed him to proceed still further to the Choḷa and Pāṇḍya countries. Accordingly Viśakhāchārya repaired to those regions and propagated the tenets of the Jaina Law among their inhabitants who were already familiar with the Jaina doctrine.

Further, on the strength of these epigraphic, archaeological and literary evidences pertaining to the last days of Bhadrabāhu and Chandragupta, the eminent historians of India and western countries also state and accept as historical fact this association of Bhadrabāhu and Chandragupta with Śravaṇa-Beḷagoḷa.

(i) Mr. B. Lewis Rice has stoutly maintained the credibility of the tradition in many publications (vide '*Inscriptions at Śravaṇa-Beḷagoḷa* and *Mysore and Coorg from the Inscriptions*, pp. 3-9).

(ii) Mr. R. Narasiṁhāchārya, the well-known archaeologist directly concerned with the archaeological survey of Śravaṇa-Beḷagoḷa, clearly states : "A dispassionate consideration of the above mentioned facts leads one to the conclusion that the Jaina tradition has some basis to stand upon. The evidence may not be quite decisive, but it may be accepted as a working hypothesis until the contrary is proved by future research" (vide "Epigraphia Carnatica", vol. II, p. 42).

(iii) A similar conclusion has been put forward by the famous historian Vincent A. Smith, after a careful consideration of all the points bearing on the subject, in the following words : "In short, the Jaina tradition holds the field, and no alternative account exists" (vide *Oxford History of India*',' pp. 75-76).

(iv) On the same lines Mr. Vincent A. Smith makes his stand very clear in another book of his, *Early History of India*, in the following terms : "In the second edition of this book I rejected that tradition and dismissed the tale as 'imaginary history'. But on reconsideration of the whole evidence and the objections urged against the credibility of the story, I am now disposed to believe that the tradition probably is true in its main outline, and that Chandragupta really abdicated and became a Jaina ascetic. The traditional narratives, of course, like all such relations, are open to much criticism, and the epigraphical support is far from conclusive. Nevertheless, my present impression is that the tradition has a solid foundation on fact." (vide *Early History of India*, Fourth Edition, p. 154).

(v) The Celebrated authority on Ancient Indian History and Jainology, Dr. A. L. Basham, affirms the strong Jaina tradition which maintains that Emperor Chadragupta was a patron of Jainism and that he abdicated the throne, became a Jaina monk and fasted to death in the manner of Jaina saints at the great Jaina temple and monastery of Śravaṇa-Beḷagoḷa in the modern Mysore. (vide *The Wonder That Was India*, pp. 52-53, and *Sources of Indian Tradition*, p. 46).

(vi) Prof. H. C. Rāychaudharī, the well-known historian of ancient India, also confirms the Jaina tradition and states as under : "It is also affirmed that when Magadha was confronted with a famine of 12 years Chandragupta abdicated in favour of a son named Siṁhasena and retired to Śravaṇa-Beḷagoḷa in Mysore with Saint Bhadrabāhu. There he starved himself to death in the Jaina fashion. Several inscriptions in Mysore dating from about 900 A.D. refer to the pair (*yugma*) Bhadrabāhu and Chandragupta." (vide *Age of the Nandas and Mauryas*, p. 165).

(vii) Dr. Rādhā Kumud Mookerji, the great authority on Mauryan and Ancient Indian History, accepts in detail the Jaina tradition. As regards the religion of Chandragupta Maurya, he states that "There is also no evidence to disprove the fact taken for granted without the need of any argument or demonstration by all Jain writers that Chandragupta became a convert to their religion. The atmosphere of Jainism had already penetrated into Pātaliputra in the time of the Nandas-who had Jain leanings and Jain ministers". (vide "Chandragupta Maurya And His Times", p. 41). Again, regarding the association of Chandragupta with Śravaṇa-Beḷagoḷa, Dr. Mookerji affirms : "There is also the unanimous Jaina tradition that Chandragupta in his old age abdicated the throne and followed the Jain Saint Bhadrabāhu to the south and settled down at a place known as Śravaṇa-Beḷagoḷa in the State of Mysore where he lived till death. The place is full of traditions, monuments and inscriptions testifying to the life of Chandragupta as an ascetic in association with Bhadrabāhu". (vide *Ancient India*, p. 150). Further, as regards the last days and the end of Chandragupta, Dr. Mookerji states, "According to very late Jain traditions, Chandragupta, in his last days, renounced the world and followed the Jain migration led by Bhadrabāhu to a place in Mysore, known as Śravaṇa-Beḷagoḷa, where some local inscriptions still perpetuate the memory of Chandragupta and Bhadrabāhu living together as saints. The hill where he lived is still known as Chandragiri, and a temple erected by him as Chandragupta-Basti. It is said that Chandragupta, in the Jain fashion, fasted unto death in this place." (vide *History and Culture of the Indian People*, Vol. II, *The Age of Imperial Unity*, p. 61).

In this way the known history of the sacred complex of Śravaṇa-Beḷagoḷa begins from as early as the 3rd century B.C. and that too with the meaningful association of the highest dignitaries of the period like Bhadrabāhu, the eighth and last 'Śrutakevalī in succession from Lord Mahāvira and Chandragupta Maurya, the first Emperor of India.

CHAPTER IV

ROYAL PATRONAGE TO ŚRAVAṆA-BEḶAGOḶA

1. THE GAṄGAS

After the rule of the Mauryas, in the 1st century A.D. Karnāṭaka did not remain under the political control of one dynasty. On the contrary, several dynasties of kings ruled for a short or long period over different areas of Karnāṭaka as follows :

1. Sātavāhanas of Pratishṭhāna : (1st to 3rd Century A.D.)
2. Kadaṁbas of Banavāsī : (3rd to 6th century A.D.)
3. Gaṅgas of Taḷakāḍ : (350 to 999 A.D.)
4. Chālukyas of Badāmi : (500 to 757 A.D.)
5. Rāshṭrakūṭas of Malkhed : (757 to 973 A.D.)
6. Chālukyas of Kalyāṇ : (10th to 12 century A.D.)
7. Kalachūris of Kalyān : (1156 to 1183 A.D.)
8. Hoysalas of Haḷebid : (1006 A.D. to 1345 A.D.)
9. Vijayanagara Empire : (1336 to 1565 A.D.)
10. Woḍeyārs of Mysore : (1399 to 1950 A.D.)
11. British Rule : (1800 to 1947 A.D.)

The sacred place of Śravaṇa-Beḷagoḷa was under the rule of these dynasties from time to time. Out of these dynasties Śravaṇa-Beḷagoḷa came into prominence under the Gaṅga dynasty, which made Jainism as its "state religion" and whose period is regarded as the "golden age of Jainism". In fact the very foundation of the Gaṅga Kingdom is attributed to the great Jaina saint Āchārya Siṁhanandā who also acted in the capacity of an adviser to Konguṇivarman I, the first Gaṅga king. Obviously, the Gaṅga dynasty, which owed its origin to the help of a Jaina Āchārya, remained staunch to the Jaina religion. As a result, numerous inscriptions dating from the 4th to the 12th century A.D. testify to the building of the Jaina temples, consecration of Jaina images of worship, hollowing out of caves for Jaina ascetics and grants to Jaina Āchāryas by the rulers of the Gaṅga dynasty. That is why Mr. Lewis Rice, the authority on Mysore history, considered them to be the principal Jaina dynasty of the south and remarked that "With Nandagiri (i.e. modern Nandi Hills) as the fort, Kuvalāla (i e., modern Kolar) as their city, Jinendra as their god and the Jain *mata* as their faith, Daḍiga and Mādhava (i.e. Gaṅga monarchs) ruled over the earth." (vide "Mysore Gazetter," Vol. I, p. 308). Mr. Rice also thinks that there must have been a considerable Jaina element in the population of Mysore at the time over when Āchārya Siṁhanandi exerted his influence to gain their acceptance of the Gaṅga rule.

In the several inscriptions and writings we get various references to the royal patronage extended to Śravaṇa-Beḷagoḷa by Gaṅga monarchs. The earliest of the Gaṅga records refer to the erection of a Basti or Jaina temple by King Śivamāra II, the son of Śrīpurusha (726-776 A.D.). Many inscriptions also refer to King Mārasiṁha (961-974 A.D.), the doyen of the Gaṅga family. He was a monarch in every sense of the term and he has been described in the inscriptions with many a sonorous title like, 'Dharmāvatāra' (i.e. religion incarnated), 'Gaṅga-Chūḍāmaṇi' (i.e. crest-jewel of the Gaṅgas), 'Gaṅgasiṁha' (i.e. lion among the Gaṅgas), etc. All these indicate the respect he commanded in his own life-time, and he seems to have fully deserved all these appellations. He also performed the annointing ceremony of the Rāshṭrakūṭa King, Indra III, thereby indicating his political power. The inscription mentions that he always maintained the doctrine of Jina and erected Bastis and Mānastambhas at various places, and the inscription ends with the statement that he relinguished the sovereignty and, keeping the vow of 'Sallekhanā' for three days in the presence of Ajita-Bhaṭṭāraka died at Bankapura in 974 A.D. Thus he exhibited the classic example of singular devotion to his faith and fully evoked the admiration of his contemporaries. The result is seen in the erection in the year 981 A.D. of the colossal image of Gommaṭeśvara by his general Chāmuṇḍa-Rāya at Śravaṇa-Beḷagoḷa, which is in itself a monument to the zeal of the Jainas during that great age.

Mārasiṁha's successor King Rājamalla IV (974-984 A.D.) continued the royal patronage to Jainism and his minister and general Chāmuṇḍa-Rāya also continued to build religious structures at Śravaṇa-Beḷagoḷa.

Further, there are some epigraphs at Śravaṇa-Beḷagoḷa which contain references to the Gaṅgas, without mentioning any particular Gaṅga king. Inscription No. 37 merely refers to the illustrious Gaṅga family and in the inscription No. 378 there is a reference to a fierce battle between the Gaṅgas and the Choḷas. Inscription No. 69 states that Gopanandi caused the Jaina religion, which had become weak, to attain the prosperity and fame which it formerly enjoyed during the time of the Gaṅga kings. The inscription No. 67 mentions in a poetical way the help received by the founder of the Gaṅga dynasty from the Jaina teacher Āchārya Siṁhanandi in establishing his power. There are also other inscriptions and literary works which refer to Āchārya Siṁhanandi as the founder of the Gaṅga kingdom. In an old commentary on the Jaina work 'Gommaṭasāra' it is stated that the Gaṅga family prospered by the blessing of Āchārya Siṁhanandi.

2. THE RĀSHTRAKŪTAS

The Rāshṭrakūṭas were a great power in South India for more than two centuries, and like the Gaṅgas of Talakāḍ, they were zealous patrons of Jainism; Jaina literature, in particular, had its golden age under their patronage. The Gaṅgas had set up this tradition before the Rāshṭrakūṭas rose to power, and the Chālukyas, who were another important dynasty sandwitched almost between the Gaṅgas and the Rāshṭrakūṭas, were also inclined to patronise Jainism. Although they were votaries of the Vedic religion, they were greatly interested in Jainism, and supported it with a big heart.

The most famous of the Rāshṭrakūṭa kings was Amoghavarsha Nṛipatuṅga (814-878 A.D.). Although involved in wars almost incessantly he was by inclination a pacifist; he was more scholarly than militant, an author by choice and a warrior by necessity. His 'Kavirājamārga', one of the oldest Kannaḍa works available today, is a work on poetics and is a masterpiece on the subject. He also wrote in Sanskrit a book entitled "Praśnottara Ratnāvalī" dealing with Jaina ethics. His teacher was Āchārya Jinasena, the celebrated author of "Ādipurāṇa", and "Pārśvābhyudaya". During Amoghavarsha's reign only 'Jayadhavalā', the great commentary on Jaina doctrines, was prepared.

King Indra IV (966-973 A.D.), the last monarch of Rāshṭrakūṭa dynasty, was also a patron of Jainism and a great warrior as seen from the various titles applied to him. But unfortunately with his defeat in 973 A.D. by the Chālukya King Tailap II, the Rāshṭrakūṭa dynasty's rule came to an end. After this defeat Indra IV retired to Śravaṇa-Beḷagoḷa and as per Inscription No. 133 he died at Śravaṇa-Beḷagoḷa by the Jaina rite of 'Sallekhanā'.

3. THE HOYSALAS

The Hoysalas, whose kingdom included modern Mysore, were staunch Jainas and their rule which spread over a period of more than three centuries (1006 to 1345 A.D.) forms the brightest chapter in the history of medieval Karnāṭaka. The rulers of the Hoysala dynasty steadfastly followed Jainism and actually patronised it because the very foundation of the Hoysala rule was laid by the efforts of a Jaina ascetic teacher. It is recorded in the inscriptions at Śravaṇa-Beḷagoḷa that the progenitor of the Hoysala dynasty was Sala, an eponymous hero, who was a devout Jaina. On a certain occasion, we are told, he went to worship at the temple of his family deity at Sosavūra. After worship he came to his ascetic teacher, Sudatta Vardhamāna, to receive religious instruction. While he was receiving instructions, a fierce tiger came out of the forest and flared at them with rage. At this the sage said to Sala with reference to the fierce tiger "Poy Sala" (i.e. strike it, Sala); and from this circumstance Sala adopted the Sage's words as his name, i.e., Poysala or Hoysala, as also the tiger crest. In this way the utterance of the Guru 'Hoy (Poy) Sala' itself became the name of the dynasty and this dynasty succeeded in expelling the Choḷas from Mysore region and in establishing its rule in the 11th century. Thus, just as the great Jaina saint Āchārya Siṁhanandi helped in establishing the Gaṅga Kingdom in the 4th century A.D. and used to give advice to Koṅguṇivarman I, the first Gaṅga king, similarly the renowned and politically conscious Jaina saint Āchārya Sudatta guided the foundation of the Hoysala kingdom in the 11th century A.D. and took a prominent part in the administration of the Hoysalas.

From the inscriptions it is clear that the first three Hoysala rulers, viz., Sala, the founder, his son Vinayāditya I (1016-1022 A.D.) and the latter's successor Nṛipa Kāma (1022-1047 A.D.) were under the spiritual guidance of Āchārya Sudatta. The fourth Hoysala ruler Vinayāditta II (1047-1098 A.D.) was a staunch devotee of the Jaina sage Śāntideva who had been respectfully mentioned in Inscription No. 67 dated 1129 A.D. at Śravaṇa-Beḷagoḷa in the following terms : "Who is able to describe 'such and such' is the ability of the ascetic Śāntideva, having worshipped whose pair of feet, the Hoysala king Vinayāditta brought the goodess of wealth to the territory under his rule ?" What King Vinayāditta II did as a Jaina, obviously on the advice of his preceptor Śāntideva, is described in a stone record found in the Gandhavāraṇa-Basti (viz., Inscription No. 143, dated 1131 A.D.) at Śravaṇa-Beḷagoḷa in the following words, "King Vinayāditta glady made any number of tanks and temples, any number of Jina shrines, any number of nāḍūs' (or districts), villages and subjects". The erection of Jaina temples by Vinayāditta, the great builder, is thus described : "The pits dug for bricks became tanks, the mountains quarried for stone became level with the ground, the roads by which the mortarcarts passed became raviness; thus did King Poysala caused Jina temples to be built." There are many inscriptions found at other places that reveal the utmost care with which King Vinayāditta II, looked after Jaina interests.

Ereyaṅga (1098-1102 A.D.), the son and successor of Vinayāditta II, was the devoted disciple of Jaina saint Gopanandi whose qualifications and achievements are graphically described in a stone inscription at Haḷe-Beḷagoḷa dated 1094 A.D. King Ereyaṅga granted villages Rāchanahaḷḷa and the Beḷagoḷa 12 for the repairs of the Bastis, i.e., temples in the holy place round the Kalbappu hill, i.e., the Kaṭavapra or Chandragiri hill at Śravaṇa-Beḷagoḷa. It is also mentioned in the inscription that saint Gopanandi with the patronage of King Ereyaṅga "caused the Jaina religion, which had for a long time been at a stand still, to attain the prosperity and fame of the Gaṅga Kings".

King Ballāḷa I (1102-1108 A.D.), the eldest son of King Ereyaṅga, was a disciple of the Jaina guru, Paṇḍitadeva Chārukirti, whose accomplishments are mentioned in stone inscriptions dated 1398 A.D. and 1432 A.D. These are the Siddheśvara basti records of Śravaṇa-Beḷagoḷa and they depict guru Chārukirti's proficiency in medicine as well. It is stated therein that "When King Ballāḷa was verily in a moribund condition through severe illness, he quickly restored him to health...Even the air that had but touched his body cured disease; was it much (then) that his medicine cured King Ballāḷa of his disease ?"

Biṭṭi-deva (1108-1142 A.D.), who later adopted the name Vishṇuvardhana, was one of the most brilliant monarchs of Karnāṭaka. He was a great king and his achievements both in war and in peace were very remarkable. Many of the notable victories which marked his rule were won by his great Jaina generals. King Vishṇuvardhana's reign was also important from the point of his continued support to Jainism inspite of his alleged conversion from Jainism to Vaishṇavism in 1116 A.D. under the influence of the great Āchārya Rāmānuja, who, to escape persecution at the hands of a Choḷa king, had taken refuge in the Hoysala country. While this legned is popular and persistant it appears unfounded as none of the numerous inscriptions of this king contains any reference to this event and even mentions the influence of Āchārya Rāmānuja on the king. Even after about 1125 A.D., when Āchārya Rāmānuja is supposed to have left Mysore region, king Vishṇuvardhana made grants to Jaina teachers like Śrīpāla Traividyāvratī and saw merit in the consecration of the image of Pārśvanātha. Another stone inscription at Beḷur dated 1129 A.D. commemorates a gift to the Basti named 'Malli Jinālaya' by the same king Vishṇuvardhana. Further, it is recorded that when the famous Pārśvanatha Jaina temple was built in the Hoysala capital city by one of his many great Jaina generals, King Vishṇuvardhana christened his sonprince Vijaya Narasimhadeva after the god Vijaya Pārśvadeva and granted the village of Javagal for a Jaina temple in the capital Dorasamudra near Haḷebid. All these records clearly reveal that King Vishṇuvardhana, whatever his patronage to Vaishṇavism may have been, continued till the end of his rule to be a pious 'Bhavya', (Jaina house-holder.)

Queen Śāntalā-Devī, the eldest and principal wife of King Vishṇuvardhana, was undoubtedly a Jaina enthusiast and played a prominent role in the history of Jainism in Karnāṭaka. The inscription No. 132 of Śravaṇa-Beḷagoḷa records the erection in 1123 A.D. of the famous temple "Savatigandhavāraṇa-Basti" on the Chandragiri Hill by Queen Śāntalā-Devī. The same inscription eulogises Queen Śāntalā-Devi thus: The eldest daughter of Mārasinga and Māchikabbe, she was to king Vishṇu the Goddess of Victory in battle, the Goddess of wealth always resting on his breast and the Goddess of Fame spreading to the remoting points of the compass the greatness of his valour." Among the epithets applied to her are : "a Bṛihaspati in discrimination, a Vāchaspati in ready wit, the cause of the elevation of the four "Samayas" or creeds, an expert in singing instrumental music and dancing, a rampart to the Jaina faith, a rutting elephant to ill-mannered co-wives ('udvritta-savatigandhavārane')." The last epithet is interesting as the temple founded by her on the Chandragiri hill was named after it, i.e., 'Savati-gandhavāraṇa Basti.' She endowed the temple with a village and certain lands, which she presented to her Jaina teacher, the saint Prabhāchandra, after washing his feet. She died in 1131 A.D. at Śivagaṅga. Her mother Māchikabbe, resolving not to survive after the death of her daughter, went to Śravaṇa-Beḷagoḷa and, fasting for one month, died by the Jaina rite of 'Sallekhanā', in the presence of her teachers, the saints Prabhāchandra, Vardhamāna and Ravichandra. In the Inscription No. 143 several verses are devoted to glorifying her self-sacrifice and severe penance.

King Narasiṁha I (1142-1173 A.D.), the third son and succcessor of Vishṇuvardhana, carried on the tradition of Hoysala kings. King Narasiṁha gave the name of "Bhavya-Chūḍāmaṇi-Basti" to the famous "Chaturviṁśati-Tīrthaṅkara-Basti" built by his General Hulla-Rāja in the village of Śravaṇa-Beḷagoḷa in the year 1159 A.D. and granted for its upkeep the village Savaneru. The temple is popularly known as "Bhaṇḍārī Basti", since Hulla-Rāja was also "Bhaṇḍārī" or treasurer of King Narasiṁha I.

King Ballāḷa II or Vīra-Ballāḷa I (1173-1220 A.D.) organised the Kingdom upon a footing of peace and prosperity and like his predecessors showed marked favour to the spread of Jainism. His titles and achievements are given in Inscriptions Nos. 327 and 335, at Śravaṇa-Beḷagoḷa. It is evident from Inscription No. 240, dated 1175 A.D., that the King gave his confirmation to the grant of three villages made by his father King Narasiṁha I for temples of Gommaṭṭa, Pārśvanātha and the twenty-four Tīrthaṅkaras. Thus King Ballāḷa II gave the village Bammeyanahaḷḷi for the temple of Pārśvanātha set up by Achlādevī, granted the village Bekka for the worship of Gommaṭeśvara, and continued the gift of village Savaneru for the upkeep of the Chaturviṁśati-Tīrthaṅkara-Basti at śravaṇa-Beḷagoḷa. Further, in 1176 A.D. a Jaina temple was built by a Jaina merchant who colled it 'Vīra-Ballāḷa Jinālaya' in honour of the king, and King Vīra-Ballāḷa I granted it a village. About twenty years later, in 1195 A.D., Nāgadeva, the minister and 'Pattaṇa-Swāmī' of Ballāḷa II, built the Nagara Jinālaya as a disciple of Nayakirti, King Ballāḷa II made a grant to this temple built at his own capital Dwarasamudra "for feeding Jaina ascetics and bringing on the eigh-fold worship of the temple."

King Narasiṁha II (1220-1235 A.D.) followed the policy of his father King Ballāḷa II. The Inscription No. 186 at Śravaṇa-Beḷagoḷa ascribes paramount titles to him and records that the king confirmed in 1231 A.D. the grant made by one Shri Gommaṭa-seṭṭī as a perpetual endowment for the worship of Gommaṭeśvara and the twenty-four Tīrthaṅkaras.

Similarly, king Narasiṁha III (1254-1292 A.D.), the grandson of King Narasiṁha II and the son of Someśvara, also confirmed the grants of land made by Saṁbhudeva and others with a view to provide milk-offerings for Gommaṭeśvara and the twenty-four Tīrthaṅkaraś temple situated in the enclosure on the Vindhyagiri hill. This king Narasiṁha III and his bro-other Rāmanātha (1254-1295 A.D.) who ruled over a section of the Hoysala Empire were devout Jainas. About King Narsiṁha III's Diety as a Jaina we have evidence in the Pārśvanātha Basti stone record found at Bastihaḷḷi near Haḷebid, the Hoysala capital. The spiritual adviser of this king was famous Jaina saint Māghanandī Siddhāntā of the Balātkāra 'gaṇa', i.e., section. This is gathered from the Bennegudda inscription at Haḷebid dated 1265 A.D. and the Nagara Jinālaya inscription at Śravaṇa-Beḷagoḷa deted 1282 A.D. In this inscription at Śravaṇa-Beḷagoḷa the saint is styled as 'Mahāmaṇḍalāchārya', best of the Āchāryas, royal 'guru' to the Hoysala king, and the emperor of philosophers. To saint Māghanandī king Narasiṁha III granted village kallangere together with fourteen hamlets attached to it for maintaining the Jaina temple called 'Trikūṭa-ratnatraya-Śāntinātha-Jinālaya'. This temple was also called 'Trikūṭaratnatraya-Nṛisiṁha-Jinālaya', obviously as a mark of esteem and loyalty to the king.

During the reigns of the last two Hoysala monarchs, viz., Ballāḷa III (1292-1343 A.D.) and Ballāḷa IV (1343-1345 A.D.) Jainism did not get as much royal patronage as it had during the reigns of all other Hoysala kings from 1006 A.D., Yet there is ample proof to show that Jainism still predominated in Karṇāṭaka in the reigns of these two rulers.

4. THE VIJAYANAGARA KINGS

Although the rulers of the Vijayanagara Empire were devotees of Vishṇu and Siva, they not only tolerated jainism but encouraged it. The finest example of this noble tradition of toleration is found in the Inscription No. 344 at Śravaṇa-Beḷagoḷa which refers to a reconciliation brought about by the Vijayanagara King Bukka-Rāya I between the 'Bhavyas', (Jainas) and the 'Bhaktas' (Vaishṇavasn) in 1368 A.D. It opens with a verse in praise of the Śrīvaishṇava apostle Rāmānujāchārya and proceeds to say that "the Jainas having made petition to the king about the injustice done to them by the Vaishṇavas, he, taking the hand of the Jainas and placing it in the hand of the Śrīvaishṇavas of the eighteen 'nāḍus' (i. e., districts) including the Āchāryas of Śrīraṅgam, Tirupati, Kāñchī and Melkote, and other Vaishṇava sects, and declaring at the same time that there was no difference between the Vaishṇava and the Jaina

'Darśanas', i.e., creeds, decreed thus : The Jaina creed is as before, entitled to the privileges of five great musical instruments and the 'Kalaśa' or vase. If loss or advancement should be caused to the Jaina creed through the Vaishṇavas, the latter will kindly deem it as loss or advancement caused to their own creed. The Śrīvaishṇavas will to this effect kindly set up a 'Sāsana' or inscription in all the 'bastis' or temples of the kingdom. For as long as the sun and moon endure the Vaishṇava creed will continue to protect the Jaina creed. The Vashṇavas and the Jainas are one (body) : they must not be viewed as different. Tātayya of Tirupati will, out of the money levied from every Jaina house throughout the kingdom, appoint twenty servants as a bodyguard for the god at Beḷagoḷa and repair ruined Jaina temples. He who transgresses this decree shall be a traitor to the king, a traitor to the 'saṅgha' and the 'Samudāya'."

The details given of the administration of this unique edict seem to show that the king Bukka Rāya I was even partial to the 'Bhavyas', as the Jainas were called, and threw the burden of their protection upon his coreligionists, the 'Bhaktas', as the Vaishṇavas were called.

Later on, this attitude of protection towards the Jainas would seem to have advanced the Jainas even a step further. For, according to Inscription No. 337 of about 1410 A.D. at Śravaṇa-Beḷagoḷa. Bhīmā-Devi, the queen of Deva-Rāya I of Vijayanagara, was a disciple of the Jaina teacher Abhinava-Chārukīrti-Paṇḍitachārya and she set up an image of Śāntinatha-Tīrthaṅkara in the Maṅgāyi Basti at the village Śravaṇa-Beḷagoḷa. Furter, Inscription No. 253 of 1422 A.D. at Śravaṇa-Beḷagoḷa refers to Iruguppa the General of Vijayanagara king Harihara II and records the grant made by him of Beḷagoḷa, together with a grove and a tank built by him, for Gommaṭeśvara. A large portion of this Inscription mentions the pedigree and praises of Irguppa. He was a Sanskrit scholar and wrote the metrical lexicon 'Nānārtharatnāmālā'. Two of his other inscriptions found in Karnāṭaka and bearing the dates 1382 A.D. and 1387 A.D. contain praises of Paṇḍitāchārya and a third inscription, dated 1385 A.D., states that Iruguppa who adhered to the doctrine of the Jaina teacher Siṁhanandi built the stone temple of Kumthu-Jinanātha at Vijayanagara,

5. THE MYSORE RULERS

Like the Gaṅgas of Taḷakāḍ and the Hoysalas of Haḷebid, the Woḍeyār kings of Mysore also extended their patronage to Jainism and always took special interest in the upkeep and proper maintenance of the shrines at Śravaṇa-Beḷagoḷa which for med a part of the Mysore kingdom. In several incriptions and literary works there are many references to the visits of Mysore kings to Śravaṇa-Beḷagoḷa, to the presence of Mysore rulers at the different grand head-annointing ceremonies of the colossal image of Lord Gommaṭeśvara and to vari ous instances of actual financial and other kinds of help readily rendered by the Mysore kings to solve the particular problems connected with the management of the properties attached to the temples in Śravaṇa-Beḷagoḷa. The best instance of this type has been recorded in the Inscription No. 250 dated 1634 A.D. It says that the great king of Mysore, Chāma-Rāja-Woḍeyār, finding that the temple lands of Beḷagoḷa had been for a long time mortgaged to certain Jaina merchants, sent for the latter and proposed to pay off the mortgage, whereupon the merchants unanimously agreed to release the mortgage as a work of merit in the presence of Gommaṭeśvara and their guru Chārukīrti-Paṇḍita. The details of this whole transaction are given in Inscription No. 352 which is a copper plate grant of 1634 A.D. This grant lays down a strict prohibition against any of the temple managers mortgaging the lands in future and against any one granting a mortgage thereon. Though the inscriptions do not expressly say so, the king must have visited Beḷagoḷa in connection with this transaction of release of mortgage of temple lands. But the literary work 'Munivaṁśābhudaya' composed by Chidānandakavi in 1680 A.D. gives several details of the king's visit to Beḷagoḷa. In this work it is specially mentioned that King Chāma-Rāja-Woḍeyār took personal interest in re-instating with due honours on the seat of Bhaṭāṭraka the former traditional guru Chārukīrti who had abandoned Śravaṇa-Beḷagoḷa and was living at Bhaṭṭātakipura (i.e. Gerusoppe) under the protection of Bhairavarāja with a view to escape from the trouble caused by the Telugu chief Jagadeva of Chennapaṭṭaṇa and that the king made a special grant to the Jaina Maṭha on this occasion.

The successors of King Chāma-Rāja-Woḍeyār also continued to extend their generous patronage and to grant rich endowments for the upkeep and worship at Śravaṇa-Beḷagoḷa.

(i) King Doḍḍa-Deva-Rāja-Woḍeyār (1659-1673 A.D.) made, as per Inscription No. 401, a grant of the village Rāgibommena haḷḷi in 1672 A.D. for the upkeep of a feeding house for the Brahmanas. The 'Sthala-purāṇa' says that he visited Beḷagoḷa in the year 1672 A.D.

(ii) King Chikka-Deva-Rāja-Woḍeyār (1673-1704 A.D.) caused, as per Inscription No. 365, the construction of the 'Kalyāṇi' (pond) at Śravaṇa-Beḷagoḷa.

(iii) King Krishṇa-Rāya-Woḍeyār I (1717-1731 A.D.), the grandson of Chikka-Deva-Rāja, as per Inscription No. 249, paid a visit to Śravaṇa-Beḷagoḷa in 1723 A.D. and made the grant of certain villages including Beḷagoḷa for the worship of Gommaṭeśvara and of the village of Kabale for the maintenance of the alms-house situated near the Chikka-Deva-Rāja pond. The inscription further states that on seeing the face of the divine Gommaṭa he was greatly pleased, and, with horripilation, made the grant.

(iv) King Krishṇa-Rāya-Woḍeyār III, as per Inscription No. 353, confirmed in 1810 A.D. the former grant of village Kabale made by Krishṇa-Rāja-Woḍeyār I. The insciption No. 354 records the grant in 1830 A.D. of three villages to provide for the expenses and repairs of all the temples at Śravaṇa-Beḷagoḷa. The number of the temples is given as thirty-three as follows :

8 on the Doḍḍa-Beṭṭa, i.e., Vindhyagiri hill, consisting of the big god Gommaṭa, and seven minor temples;
16 on the Chikka-Beṭṭa, i.e., Chandragiri Hill,
8 in the village Beḷagoḷa, and
1 on the hill at Maleyur.

It is also stated that formerly the 'Maṭha' or monastery was in receipt of a cash grant of only 120 'varāhas' to meet all these expenses; and as the amount was found insufficient, the present grant of three villages was made in lieu of the former cash grant. Further, the king got the grand head-annointing festival of Gommaṭeśvara performed in 1827 A.D.

(v) King Krishṇa-Rāya-Woḍeyār IV paid his first visit to Śravaṇa-Beḷagoḷa on 10th November 1900, and this visit is indicated by his initials K.R.M. engraved on the summit of Chikka-Beṭṭa, i.e., the Chandragiri Hill. Further, the king got three grand head-annointing festivals of Gommaṭeśvara performed in succession on (a) the 30th or March, 1910, (b) the 15th of March, 1925, and (c) the 26th of February, 1940. The grand festival of 1940 A.D. was very significant, in the sense that it was completely arranged for the first time by the Mysore Government—while all the earlier festivals were arranged by the Jaina community—and that the later festivals held on the 5th of Maɹch 1953 and on the 30th of March 1967 were also organised by the Karnāṭaka Government in close co-operation with the Jaina community.

CHAPTER V

CHĀMUṆDA-RĀYA AND ŚRAVAṆA-BEḶAGOḶA

1. PRE-EMINENT POSITION

Just as the benevolent kings of various dynasties that ruled over different areas of Karnāṭaka from the ancient times generously extended their royal patronage for the proper upkeep and adequate maintenance of the holy place of Śravaṇa-Beḷagoḷa, similarly their Chief Ministers and Military Generals also took personal and special interest not only in giving sufficient protection to Śravaṇa-Beḷagoḷa in the days of turmoil and disturbances but also in continuously enhancing the sanctity and importance of Śravaṇa-Beḷagoḷa by incessantly making varied and rich contributions of an enduring nature. Among such note-worthy Chief Ministers and Military Generals of Karnāṭaka, Chāmuṇḍa-Rāya of the Gaṅga Kingdom and Gaṅga-Rāja and Hulla-Rāja of the Hoysala Empire stand out very prominently in the history of Śravaṇa-Beḷagoḷa and in the promotion of Jaina religion. The extremely pre-eminent position of these three great Ministers in the field of Jaina religious activities has been quite distinctly recorded in Inscription No. 345 dated 1160 A.D. at Śravaṇa-Beḷagoḷa in the following words:

"If it be asked who at the beginning were the firm promoters of the Jaina doctrine,—only Rāya (i.e.—Chāmuṇḍa-Rāya), the excellent minister of Rāchamalla, after him, only Gaṅga-Rāja, the excellent minister of King Viśṇu; and after him again, only Hulla, the excellent minister of king Narasiṁha. If any other had such claim, why not name him?"

This record clearly indicates that these three Generals and Ministers, viz.,

(i) Chāmuṇḍa-Rāya of Gaṅga King Rājamalla IV (974-984 A.D.),
(ii) Gaṅga-Rāja of Hoysala king Vishṇuvardhana (1108-1142 A.D.), and
(iii) Hulla-Rāja of Hoysala monarch Narasiṁha I (1142-1173 A.D.)

were mainly responsible for the promotion of Jaina religion. That is why Chāmuṇḍa-Rāja Gaṅga-Rāja and Hulla-Rāja are described as the triumvirate of pre-eminent promoters of the Jaina faith.

Among these three benefactors of Jaina religion, however, the contributions of Chāmuṇḍa-Rāya are by far of the most outstanding, inspiring and lasting nature. By his rich personal accomplishments and varied achievements in different fields Chāmuṇḍa-Rāya has made a permanent mark and there is hardly any other personality of his stature and competence in the history of Karnāṭaka. Chāmuṇḍa-Rāya has emerged into the light of history of Karnāṭaka as a faithful minister, a loyal General, a profound scholar and a great patron of Jainism. That is why the famous historian of Karnāṭaka Dr. B.A. Saletore refers to the pre-eminent position of Chāmuṇḍa-Rāya in the following terms. "The first great name in the constellation of brilliant Jaina Generals we meet with is that of Chāmuṇḍa-Rāya, popularly known as Rāya. A braver soldier, a more devout Jaina, and a more honest man than Chāmuṇḍa-Rāya Karnāṭaka had never seen."

2. MILITARY VICTORIES

Even though Chāmuṇḍa-Rāya held such a pre-eminent position in Karnāṭaka and had such a remarkable record of achievements in different fields to his credit, still it is unfortunate that very little information about his personal life is available. The details about his native place, parents, place of birth, childhood, education, early career etc. are not known. Luckily in the Sanskrit work entitled "*Bhujabali-Charitra*" depicting the life-story of Bāhubali or Gommaṭa, there are some stray refeerences about Chāmuṇḍa-Rāya's life. It is known that Chāmuṇḍa-Rāya's mother's name was Kālaḷa-Devī, his wife's name was Ajitā-Devī and his son's name was Jina-Deva and that he had one younger sister by name Pullauā and one younger brother by name Nāgavarmā. Again, from this source and also from inscriptions it is learnt that Chāmuṇḍa-Rāya belonged to a Brāhma-Kshātra family. It means that he was a Brahmin by birth and became a Kshatriya or warrior by profession. Since he excelled in his work and achievements he was termed as "*Brāhma-Kshātra-Kula-maṇī*", i.e., the gem of Brāhma-Kshātra family and as "*Brāhma-Kshātra-Kula-Bhānu*", i.e., the sun of Brāhma-Kshātra family. By sheer dint of merit Chāmuṇḍa-Rāya rose to the position of the Military General and Chief Minister in the Gaṅga Kingdom and later on he was placed in charge of 'Madhurā' the southern region of the Gaṅga kingdom. He spent most of his life at Taḷakāḍ, the capital city of the Gaṅga Kingdom. As he enjoyed a long life he had the rare opportunity to serve as General and Minister to the three Gaṅga monarchs in succession, viz., Mārasiṁha (961-974 A.D.), Rājamalla IV (974-984 A.D.) and Rakkasa-Gaṅga. In his life he always held in high esteem his God 'Jina', his master 'Gaṅga Monarch', his preceptor 'Āchārya Nemichandra' and his mother 'Kālala-Devī' and devoted his entire life and directed all his activities to secure their blessings and admiration.

As the Commander-in-Chief of his Kingdom Chāmuṇḍa-Rāya proved his merit and had many military victories to his credit. In recognition of his superb skill in warfare and his successes, various coveted titles, which were generally borne by the kings, were awarded to him. When the western Chālukya opposition led by prince Rājāditya posed a formidable danger to the safety of the Gaṅga kingdom, Chāmuṇḍa-Rāya defeated Rājāditya by attacking the fortress of Ucchaṅgī, where Rājāditya had shut himself. The stone inscription dated 974 A.D. found on the Kuge Brahmadeva Pillar on the Vindhyagiri hill at Śravaṇa-Beḷagoḷa relates the siege of Ucchaṅgī and states that the this storming of famous fortress by Chāmuṇḍa-Rāya astonished the world. In this way the credit of annihilating the Western Chālukya danger to the very existence of the Gaṅga Kingdom goes to Chāmuṇḍa-Rāya and for the valour shown in this brave fight he received the title of "*Raṇaraṅga-siṅgha*" or "*Raṇa-Rāja-siṁha*", i.e., 'a great lion in battle', which was borne by the vanquished prince Rājāditya. This victory was won during the reign of Gaṅga king Rājamalla IV.

Like Western Chālukyas, the Nolaṁbas also had posed a

serious threat to the Gaṅga kingdom. In answer to this grave challenge Chāmuṇḍa-Rāya attacked the Nolaṁbas and crushed their army in the fierce battle fought on the plain of Goṇūr. For the valour which Chāmuṇḍa-Rāya displayed it this war, he was given the title of "*Vīramārtaṇḍa*", i.e., 'the sun among the brave', Inscription No. 281, dated about 983 A.D. at Śravaṇa-Beḷagoḷa gives the details of this war and relates how the Gaṅga king praised Chāmuṇḍa-Rāya for his victory against Nolaṁba king.

Other enemies of the Gaṅga kingdom were likewise very formidable, but they too suffered the same fate at the hands of this indomitable Jaina General. In these various wars decisive victories were won by him and he was awarded aspecific title for his success in each war as follows :

i) "*Samara-Dhuraṁdhara*", i.e., 'the leader', for inflicting a defeat on Vijjala-deva in the Kheḍaga war;

(ii) "*Vairikula-kāladaṇḍa*", i.e., 'the sceptre of death for the hosts of enemies', for killing Tribhuvana Vīra and others in the fort of Bagalūr and enabling Govinda to enter it;

(iii) "*Bhuja-Mārtaṇḍa*", i.e. 'the sun among the powerfull-armed', for defeating Rāja Basa, Śivara, Kuṇaka, and other warriors in the fort of King Kāma;

(iv) "*Samara-Paraśurāma*", i.e., 'Paraśurāma in battle', for slaying Mudurāchārya known as Chalaṇdaka-Gaṅga and Gaṅgara-Bhata who killed his younger brother Nāgavarmā;

(v) "*Pratipaksha-Rākshasa*" for his skill in destroying the enemies; and

(vi) "*Bhaṭa-mārī*" for destroying the fort of the warrior (i.e. bhaṭa) Vīra.

Apart from superb military leadership, Chāmuṇḍa-Rāya displayed his administrative capacity as a Minister also. During his period the Gaṅga kingdom registered steady progress in several nation-building and cultural activities. The prosperity of the people, construction of temples and installation of the colossal image of Gommaṭeśvara at Śravaṇa-Beḷagoḷa give eloquent testimony to the peace time leadership of Minister Chāmuṇḍa-Rāya.

3. LITERARY ACHIEVEMENTS

Just as Chāmuṇḍa-Rāya was superb as a warior, he was

equally great as a scholar and author, It appaars that he received thorough education during his early career in life and that he specially maintained his interest in academic and literary pursuits throughout his life. He had gained mastery over Kannaḍa language and was equally proficient in classical languages like Sanskrit and Prakrit. He was awarded the title of '*Kavijana-śekhara*' by his contemporaries.

As an author, Chāmuṇḍa-Rāya has to his credit some of the celebrated works in Sanskrit and Kannaḍa as follows :

(i) *Charitrasāra* : It is a scholarly treatise written in Sanskrit on the subject of the practices of ascetics. This book has recently been published.

(ii) *Commentary on Gommaṭasāra* : Ācharya Nemichandra, the preceptor of Chāmuṇḍa-Rāya, wrote in Prakrit an authoritative work on Jain Philosophy and titled it as "Gommṭasāra" in token of his love for his disciple Chāmuṇḍa-Rāya who was affectionately known by the term 'Gommaṭa', i.e., the beautiful. Chāmuṇḍa-Rāya worte a commentary on 'Gommaṭasāra' in the Kannaḍa language and it is reported that he did so in the presence of Āchārya Nemichandra who was popularly known by the honorific title 'Siddhānta Chakravartī'. In the last verse of 'Gommaṭasāra' there is a reference to the fact that Chāmuṇḍa-Rāya wrote in the popular language a commentary named '*Vīra-mārtaṇḍī*'. One of the titles of Chāmuṇḍa-Rāya being 'Vīra mārtaṇḍa', he named his commentary 'Vīra Mārtaṇḍī', meaning 'composed by Vīramārtaṇḍa'. This commentary of Chāmuṇḍa-Rāya seems to have been lost. It is stated that the famous commentator Keśava Varṇī had based his 'Commentary on Gommaṭasāra' on Chāmuṇḍa-Rāya's Kannaḍa Commentary. This is clear from the fact that in the opening Verses of this '*Keśavavarṇīya Vritti*' the author says : "I write the 'Vritti on Gommaṭasara' from the Karnāṭaka Vritti".

(iii) *Trishashṭilakshaṇa-Mahāpurāṇa* : Chāmuṇḍa-Rāya wrote in Kannaḍa the prestigeous book entitled "Trishashṭilakshaṇa-Mahāpurāṇa" which is better known as "*Chāmuṇḍarāya-Purāṇa*". This Kannaḍa masterpiece gives in beautiful language a biographical sketch of sixty three celebrated persons of Jaina faith. This work is mostly in Kannaḍa prose and occasionally verses in Sanskrit, Prakrit and Kannaḍa also occur. This work is of special interest and importance in the history of Kannaḍa literature as the work of the great Minister and General who erected the famous colossus of Gommaṭeśvara at Śravaṇa-Beḷagoḷa, and also as the oldest extant specimen of a book written in continuous prose, enabling us, therefore, to gain a knowledge of the language as spoken in the 10th century A.D. since this prose classic was written in 978 A.D. Apart from the point of view of language, this work is significant from the point of view of the subject also, as it is the oldest work in Kannaḍa literature depicting the lives of sixty-three great celebrities of the Jaina faith. Further, this work is also interesting from the historical point of view, as we find reference to Chāmuṇḍa-Rāya's own life and to his contemporary saints, kings and poets. Both the opening and concluding chapters of this 'purāṇa' give a few important and valuable detailed information. In this work Chāmuṇḍa-Rāya has paid his heartfelt regards to his esteemed teacher Āchārya Ajitaseṇa. He has also shown very high respects to his another teacher Āchārya Nemichandra, who was a great voluminous writer in Prakrit language.

It is really significant to note that in all his writings Chāmuṇḍa-Rāya invariably adopted the prose style in preference to verse because the very aim of his writings was to convey to common masses the basic principles and important personalities of Jaina faith in as simple and easy terms as possible. It is stated by many critics of Kannaḍa literature like Govinda Pai and others that Chāmuṇḍa-Rāya had no desire to establish himself as a poet but on the contrary wanted to be a popular writer on religion. That is why Chāmuṇḍa-Rāya's personality as a literary figure has commanded respect by his successors. Many other Kannaḍa writers have paid their high tributes and respectful reverence to him. Chāmuṇḍa-Rāya has also influenced a good number of Kannaḍa writers.

In addition to his literary character, Chāmuṇḍa-Rāya has also helped other writers and poets like Ranna, one of the triumvirate of the poets of Kannaḍa literature. Out of Paṁpa (the author of '*Ādipurāṇa*'), Ponna (the author of '*Śāntināṭha-purāṇa*') and Ranna (the author of '*Ajitanātha-purāṇa*'), the three great Jaina poets of the 10th Century A.D., who are also called '*Ratnatrayas*' (i.e. the three jewels) and '*Jinasamayadīpakār*' (i.e. the beacon light of Jaina philosophy), the poet Ranna got full support and encouragement from Chāmuṇḍa-Rāya. When

Ranna or Ratnākara migrated from his native place in North Karnaṭaka to Taḷakāḍa, the capital of the Gaṅga kingdom, in search of help for his higher education and encouragement for his poetic talents, Chāmuṇḍa-Rāya was very much impressed by Ranna's literary abilities and keen desire for learning. Since Chāmuṇḍa-Rāya had always cherished a high regard for learning, he extended all help to Ranna. As a result, Ranna developed into a great poet and was considered as one of the '*Kavi-ratnatrayas*', The Gaṅga King Tailapa was so much moved by Ranna's poetic works that he awarded to poet Ranna the coveted title of "*Kavi-Chakravartī*", In this way poet Ranna's eminent position in Indian literature was mainly due the constant patronage of minister Chāmuṇḍa-Rāya. That is why it is aptly said that Chāmuṇḍa-Rāya made two great and lasting contributions to Indian culture : one, the statue of Gommaṭeśvara and, two, the poet Ranna.

4. PROMOTION OF JAINISM

Apart from being a courageous warrior, a benevolent minister, a brilliant scholar, a patron of learning and a reputed author, Chāmuṇḍa-Rāya was also a devout Jaina. He had firm faith in the Jaina religion and he always tried to lead his life strictly according to its tenets. He used to perform scrupulously the six essential duties like worship of God, service of saints, reading of scriptures, etc., prescribed in Jaina religious books for the observance by the Jaina householders. In fact, all the members of his family, viz., his mother Kālala-Devī, his wife Ajita-Devī, his son Jina-Deva, his younger sister Pullavā, and his younger brother Nāga-Varmā, were extremely religious-minded and invariably took pride in conducting their entire behaviour strictly in accordance with the rules of conduct laid down in Jaina scriptures. Further, Chāmuṇḍa-Rāya had a keen desire from his childhood to have a perfect understanding of the fundamental principles of Jainism and to undertake an intensive study of authoritative Jaina sacred books under the constant guidance of the most able Jain ascetic '*gurus*', of his time. For fulfilling this desire he spared no pains and carried out his religious studies under a number of able and proficient gurus whose names are mentioned in the contemporary inscriptions and literature as follows :

(i) In '*Chāmuṇḍa-Rāya-Purāṇa*' : Chandrikāvata, Dharma-sena, Kumāra-sena of Mulguda and Kopana, Nāga-sena, Vīra-sena, Chandra-sena, Ārya-nandī, Ajita-sena, the disciple of Naya-sena.

(ii) In '*Charitrasāra*' : Jina-sena.

(iii) In '*Gommaṭasāra*' : Ajita-sena, Ārya-sena, Indra-nandī, Kanaka-nandī, Abhaya-nandī and Vīra-nandī.

In addition to these 'gurus', Chāmuṇḍa-Rāya was intensely attached to Āchārya Nemichandra, the most renowned Jaina ascetic preceptor of the time. Āchārya Nemichandra was awarded the title of "*Siddhānta-Chakravartī*", because he had conquered all the realms of the known knowledge of the sacred books. He was called the Chakravartī or Emperor because just as a Chakravartī monarch conquers six parts of the country by his Chakra weapon, similarly he had mastered the six parts of the famous authoritative work entitled '*Dhavalā*' by his weapon of intellect. His title is justified by his well known books (i) *Dravya-Saṅgraha*, (ii) *Gommaṭasāra-Jīva-kāṇḍa*, (iii) *Gommaṭa-sāra-Karma kāṇḍa* (iv) *Labdhi-sāra*, (v) *Kshapaṇā-sāra and* (iv) *Triloka-sāra*. It has been very specifically stated that out of these books Āchārya Nemichandra composed "Gommaṭasāra" according to the desire of his disciple Chāmuṇḍā-Rāya, who wished to learn the exposition of substances as enumerated in the canonical works of the Jainas. Further, Āchārya Nemichandra named the book as "Gommaṭa-sāra" because it was composed for the reading of Chāmuṇḍa-Rāya who was also known as Gommaṭa-Rāya. In fact, Āchārya Nemichandra himself, in this work has praised 'Gommaṭa-Rāya or simply Rāya which is but another name of Chāmuṇḍa-Rāya. This very intimate preceptor-disciple relationship between Āchārya Nemichandra and Chāmuṇḍa-Rāya. was so well-known that it was represented in paintings also. In a very old illuminating manuscript of '*Trilokasāra*', composed by Āchārya Nemichandra, we have a picture representing Chāmuṇḍa-Rāya, with several courtiers hearing the tenets of Jainism as expounded by Āchārya Nemichandra.

Moreover, in appreciation of his strict religious behaviour and superb moral qualities Chāmuṇḍa-Rāya was awarded the following honorific titles :

(i) '*Satya-Yudhishṭhira*', i.e. Yudhishṭhira in speaking the truth, for his quality of never telling an untruth even in jest;

(ii) *'Guṇavaṁ-kāva'*, for his steadfastness to good morals and for upholding the brave qualities of others;

(iii) *'Samyaktva-Ratnākara'*, for his unswerving self-sacrifice and for other virtues;

(iv) *'Shauchā-bharaṇa'*, for his not coveting the wealth or wives of others;

(v) *'Subhaṭa-Chudāmanī'*, for his being the head of the bravest;

(vi) *'Kavijana-Śekhara'*, for his being the head of the poets; and

(vii) *'Aṇṇā'*, for his fraternal affection to his co-religionists.

Furthermore, Chāmuṇḍa-Rāya is known not merely as a devout Jaina but also as a firm promoter of the Jaina faith. In fact, Chāmuṇḍa-Rāya's invaluable, enduring and many sided works in the religious field have made him more famous in comparison to his achievements in other fields. There are authentic records to show that with the advance of his age, Chāmuṇḍa-Rāya devoted himself mostly to religion, under his spiritual teachers Ajitasena and Nemichandra, and became immortal as one of the greatest promoters of Jaina religion by erecting images, temples, pillars, doorways, etc. and by devoting the greater part of his wealth to the worship of these images and to the maintenance of these religious structures. Chāmuṇḍa-Rāya's prominent contributions in this field are :

(1) *Gommaṭa Colossus :* Chāmuṇḍa-Rāya caused the colossal image of Gommaṭeśvara to be set up on the Vindhyagiri hill at Śravaṇa-Beḷagoḷa in the year 981 A.D.. Inscriptions of the eleventh century A.D. and of a later date and the evidence of later Jaina writers confirm this fact. (The details about the installation of this monolithic statue and its characteristic features and importance are given in chapters VI, VII and X)

(2) *Neminātha Temple* : It was on the Chandragiri hill at Śravaṇa-Beḷagoḷa that Chāmuṇḍa-Rāya erected in 982 A.D. a magnificent temple containing the image of the 22nd Jaina Tīrthaṅkara, Neminātha. Subsequently, the upper storey of the building was added by Jina-Deva, the son of Chāmuṇḍa-Rāya and an image of the 23rd Jaina Tīrthaṅkara, Pārśvanātha, was installed in it in the year 995 A.D.. Both the storeys give a fine idea of the beautiful architecture of that age. This temple is

popularly known as *Chāmuṇḍa-Rāya-Basti.*

(3) *Tyāgada Brahmadeva Pillar* : As per inscription No. 281 this elegantly carved pillar was erected by Chāmuṇḍa-Rāya and is situated outside the enclosure on the Vindhyagiri hill at Śravaṇa-Beḷagoḷa. This pillar is popularly known as "Pillar of gifts" since at this place on the hill gifts were distributed.

(4) *Akhaṇḍa-Bāgalu* : It is a doorway entrance carved out of a single rock and is situated outside the enclosure on the Vindhyagiri hill. According to tradition this door-way was caused to be made by Chāmuṇḍa-Rāya.

(5) *Brahmadeva Pillar :* This pillar with a pavillion at the top, about 6 feet above the ground level, enshrines a seated figure of Brahmadeva. It is situated just near the enclosure on the Vindhyagiri hill and was caused to be erected, as per tradition, by Chāmudṇa-Rāya.

(6) *Gullakāyaji Figure :* Below the pavillion of this Brahmadeva Pillar stands the figure, about 5 feet high, of the old and devoted woman named Gullakāyajji. According to tradition this figure also was caused to be made by Chāmuṇḍa-Rāya.

It is clear that these endowments made by Chāmuṇḍa-Rāya for the cause of Jainism have earned for him an undying name in the history of India. His entire life was a saga of dedication for the promotion of Jaina faith. His entire family scrupulously followed the path of Jainism and set an example to be emulated by others. His mother Kālada-Devī and his wife Ajita-Devi were pillars of strength for him and they extended all co-operation to him in his varied religious activities. His son Jina-Deva was also a devoted disciple of Āchārya Ajita-Sena and in keeping with the family tradition installed the image of Pārśvanātha Tīrthaṅkara in the upper storey of the Neminātha Temple on the Chandragiri hill. His younger sister Pullavā was a faithful follower of Jaina religion and died by the orthodox Jaina rite of 'Sallekhanā', in the Chandranātha temple at Vijaya mangalam in Coimbatore district.

After a very hectic and eventful career Chāmuṇḍa-Rāya died by about 990 A.D., during the reign of the Gaṅga monarch Rakkasa-Gaṅga, the successor of Rājamalla IV. It was unfortunate that Chāmuṇḍa-Rāya had to leave this world only after 9 years of his making outstanding contribution to world culture, that is, the installation of the colossal image of Gommaṭeśvara in the year 981 A.D. But it is pertinent to note that Chāmuṇḍa-Rāya's dedicated service to the cause of Jaina religion did not go in vain. Chāmuṇḍa-Rāya's monumental works provided continuous inspiration for centuries. As a result we find that renowned Military Generals and Chief Ministers like Gaṅga-Rāja and Hulla-Rāja of the Hoysala Empire continued with zeal the work of Chāmuṇḍa-Rāya during the 12th century at Śravaṇa-Beḷagoḷa.

5. INSPIRATION TO GAṄGA-RĀJA AND HULLA-RĀJA

Among the ministers who made valuable and lasting contributions to promote Jaina religion in general and to enhance the sanctity of Śravaṇa-Beḷagoḷa in particular, the names of Chāmuṇḍa-Rāya, Gaṅga-Rāja and Hulla-Rāja are invariably grouped together. In fact, Inscription No. 345 at Śravaṇa-Beḷagoḷa mention them as forming the triumvirate of pre-eminent promoters of the Jaina faith. It means that the policy followed and the works undertaken by Chāmuṇḍa-Rāya for the cause of Jaina faith at Śravaṇa-Beḷagoḷa during the 10th century, were continued with vigour and zeal by Gaṅga-Rāja and Hulla-Rāja, the Hoysala ministers, during the 12th century.

Gaṅga-Rāja, also known as Gaṅga, Gaṅgana, and Gaṅga-aypa, was Military General and Chief Minister of the Hoysala monarch Vishṇuvardhana (1108-1142 A.D.). From the time of his great grand father Nāgavarmā, who belonged to Kauṇḍiṇya Gotra of the Brāhmaṇa Varṇa, the observance of Jaina religion was an established family tradition, Gaṅga-Rāja's father Echa alias Budhamitra, who worked as General and Minister to Hoysala king Nṛipakāma, was a devout Jaina and a disciple of saint Kanaka-nandī of Mallur in Coorg area. Similarly, Pochikabbe alias Pochalā-Devī, the mother of Gaṅga-Rāja, was a staunch follower of Jainism, she made several religious endowments at Śravaṇa-Beḷagoḷa and other places and ultimately left this world in 1121 A.D., by the Jaina rite of 'Sallekhanā'. On the same lines General Gaṅga-Rāja and his talented wife Lakshmī-Devī continued their patronage to Jainism under the guidance of their saint preceptor Śubha-Chandra Siddhānta-deva.

Gaṅga-Rāja was a brave warrior and an able General. Inscriptions Nos. 73, 125, 240, 251 and 397 at Śravaṇa-Beḷagoḷa give an eloquent account of Gaṅga-Rāja's achievements and even discribe him as a hundred-fold more fortunate than the former Rāya of the Gaṅgas, that is, Chāmuṇḍa-Rāya. Through his superb military strategies Gaṅga-Rāja inflicted crushing defeats on armies of Chālukya, Gaṅga, Choḷa and other enemies and thus paved the way for Hoysala supremacy. In appreciation of his valour and various benevolent activities, Gaṅga-Rāja was awarded several titles which are mentioned in Inscription No. 118 dated 1120 A.D. as follows :

"Obtainer of the band of five great instruments; '*Mahā-Sāmantādhipati* : '*Mahā-Prachaṇḍa-Daṇḍanāyaka* ; Terrifier of his enemies; Purifier of his family; friend of the learned; A moon in raising the volume of the ocean of milk of the Jaina religion; A mine to the jewel perfect faith in Jainism; Taker of delight in gifts of food, shelter, medicine and learning; '*Śvāmīdroha-gharaṭṭa*', i.e., a millstone to traitors of his lord'; A foundation pillar for supporting the mansion of Dharma".

Gaṅga-Rāja was also a successful minister. How helpful he was to his lord is poetically described in an inscription thus : "As the thunderbolt to Indra, as the plough to Balarāma, as the discus to Vishṇu, as the spear to Subrahmaṇya, as the bow Gaṇḍīva to Arjuna, even so, does Gaṅga-Rāja conduct the affairs of King Vishṇu".

In addition to his military successes and benevolent administration, Gaṅga-Rāja has to his credit a number of religious activities which greatly increased the importance of Śravaṇa-Beḷagoḷa as a sacred place. In this respect Gaṅga-Rāja is very favourably compared with Chāmuṇḍa-Rāya in an inscription at Śravaṇa-Beḷagoḷa in the following terms :

"The Kunda-Kunda line of the Mūla-Saṅgha is the most ancient in the Jaina creed; and the promoter of that line is undoubtedly the General Gaṅga-Rāja, lay disciple of Śubhachandra-Siddhāntadeva... Wherever he marched, wherever he was encamped, wherever his eyes rested, wherever his mind was attracted, there he had Jina temples made; and thus the country was everywhere brought through Gaṅga-Rāja to the condition in which it had been in days of yore. After Chāmuṇḍa-Rāya he was the chief promoter of the Jaina doctrine".

Supernatural power was also attributed to him; for it is stated that just as the river Godāwarī stopped flowing on account of the Jaina devotee Attimabbarasi, the river Kāverī, though it swelled and surrounded Gaṅga-Rāja, did not touch him, thus testifying to the depth of his devotion to the Jaina faith.

Gaṅga-Rāja made the following major contributions in the religious field to Śravaṇa-Beḷagoḷa.

(1) *Construction of enclosure around Gommaṭa image :* Gaṅga-Rāja built a heavy wall at some distance around the colossal image of Gommaṭeśvara. This high solid wall built in 1117 A. D. has made the area around the image on the Vindhyagiri hill into a compact enclosure. By this wall the overall impressiveness of the image from a long distance is reduced to some extent. But it appears that the marvellous image of Gommaṭeśvara needed such protection from the attacks of sectarian fanatics.

(2) *Grant of village Govindavāḍī :* In inscriptions Nos. 240, 251 and 397 it is stated that Gaṅga-Rāja, after his victory over the Choḷa feudatories at Ṭaḷakāḍ, obtained as a boon from the king Vishṇuvardhana the village of Govindavāḍī and granted it for the worship of Gommaṭeśvara.

(3) *Erection of Śāsana-Basti :* It is recorded in inscription No. 74 that Gaṅga-Rāja erected the Jina temple, Indirākula-gṛha, now known as the Śāsana-Basti due to the inscription set up conspicuously at its entrance. The temple was built in 1117 A.D. in the middle of the Temple Sector area on the Chandragiri hill.

(4) *Erection of the Kattale-Basti :* It is recorded in inscription No. 70 that Gaṅga-Rāja erected this temple for his mother Pochavvā or Pochalā-Devī. This temple is dedicated to Ādinātha, the Ist Tīrthaṅkara, but it is popularly known as the Kattale-Basti, i e., the temple of darkness, due to lack of sufficient light in the temple. The temple was built in 1118 A.D. in the middle of the Temple Sector area on the Chandragiri hill at Śravaṇa-Beḷagoḷa.

(5) *Foundation of village Jinanāthapura :* Gaṅga-Rāja founded a new village at a distance of about one mile to the north of Śravaṇa-Beḷagoḷa and named it as 'Jinanāthapura' in the year 1117 A.D. The village became famous for its beautiful Śāntinātha-Basti erected round about 1200 A.D. by Rāchimayyā, who was minister to Hoysala King Ballāḷa II (1173-1220 A.D.).

(6) *Renovation of temples of Gaṅgavādī :* Gaṅga-Rāja restored innumerable ruined Jaina temples in all places to their former condition and thus converted the 'Gaṅgavadī into a sacred place like Kopana, situated near Hampi, the capital of Vijayanagara Empire. Inscription No. 124 at Belur says : "whatever else might be said, the myriads of ruined Jaina temples restored and built again, and the many ways in which his unbounded gifts were made, caused the Gaṅgavādī to shine like Kopana through Gaṅga-Rāja".

(7) *Grant of Village Parama :* From inscriptions No. 73 and 125 it is learnt that when Gaṅga-Rāja, after his victory over the Chālukya army at Kannegal, presented to King Vishṇuvardhana the stores and vehicles of the enemy captured in battle, the King, being pleased with his prowess, said : "I am pleased; ask for a boon", whereupon Gaṅga-Rāja asked for and obtained from the king the village of Parama and granted it to the Jina temples erected by his mother Pochalā-Devī and his wife Lakshmī-Devī.

(8) *Help in erecting Eraḍukaṭṭe-Basti :* Inscription No. 130 states that Lakshmī-Devī, the wife of Gaṅga-Rāja and a lay disciple of Śubhachandra, caused the Jina temple now known as the Eraḍukaṭṭe-Basti to be built in 1118 A.D. The temple is said to belong to the Pustaka-gachcha of the Deśiga-gaṇa of the Mūla-saṅgha, The inscription further describes Lakshmi-Devī as Chelanā in the worship of Jina, and as the lady of Policy in business and the lady of Victory in battle to Gaṅga-Rāja. This temple is dedicated to Ādinātha, the Ist Tīrthaṅkara, but is popularly known as Eraḍukaṭṭe-Basti on account of the two stairs in the east and west of the approach to it. The temple is situated on the eastern side of the Temple Sector area on the Chandragiri hill.

(9) *Help in erecting Śāntinātha Temple :* Gaṅga-Rāja encouraged his son General Boppaṇṇa to build a temple at Kambad Haḷḷi, a village situated at 11 miles away from Śravaṇa-Beḷagoḷa. Accordingly Boppaṇṇa built the temple and dedicated it to Śāntinātha, the 16th Tīrthaṅkara. The temple is popularly known as the Śāntīśvara-Basti and it is thought that its construction work must have been completed after the death of Gaṅga-Rāja.

(10) *Help in the erection of a Temple at Sāṇe-haḷḷi :* Due to encouragement of Gaṅga-Rāja, Jakkimavve, the wife of his elder brother, built in 1120 A.D. a Jina temple at Sāṇe-haḷḷi, a village situated about three miles from Śravaṇa-Beḷagoḷa. Since the temple is known as 'Haḷe Basti', i.e., old temple.

Thus General Gaṅga-Rāja's eventful career was fully devoted to the cause of the Jaina faith right upto the end of his life. From inscription No. 124 at Belur we learn that Gaṇga-Rāja died in 1133 A.D., and that his son General Boppa erected the Pārśvanātha-Basti, naming it 'Drohagharaṭṭa-Jinālaya' after one of the titles of his father to his memory at Haḷebid, the capital of Hoysala empire.

Gaṇga-Rāja's tradition of extending support to Jaina religion-was ably continued by Military General and Chief Minister Hulla.Rāja of Hoysala king Narasiṁha I (1142-1173 A.D. Minister Hulla-Rāja also known as Hulla, Hullappa or Hulla-Mayya, had a unique distinction to serve in this high office to three Hoyala kings in succession. Hulla-Rāja started his service as a minister under king Vishṇuvardhana (1108-1142 A.D.), became Chief Minister under king Narasiṁha I (1142-1173 A.D.) and continued to work in that capacity under king Ballāḷa II (1173-1220 A.D.).

Hulla-Rāja was always held in high esteem by Hoysala kings and people alike. It is stated in inscriptions that General Hulla-Rāja was minister to the king as Bṛhaspatī was to Indra : It is further stated of Hulla-Rāja that he was cleverer than Yaogandhanarāyaṇa in the management of affairs and superior to Bṛhaspatī in the knowledge of politics. Further in regard to the protection of the Hoysala Empire, Hulla-Rāja has been mentioned in the inscriptions as "*Abhīnava-Gaṅga-Rāja*", i.e., modern Gaṇga-Rāja.

Hulla-Rāja belonged to a devout Jaina family, He was a lay disciple of saint Nayakīrti Siddhānta-Deva and devotee of Mahāmaṇḍalāchārya Deva-Kīrti. Like Chāmuṇḍa-Rāya and Gaṅga-Rāya, Hulla-Rāja also worked strenously as a promoter of Jaina faith. Hulla-Rāja's major contributions to Jaina religion as given in inscriptions, may be narrated in brief as follows :

1. He renovated Uppattayata's Jina temple at Baṇkāpura, which had gone to complete ruin,

2. He caused to be built as high as kailāśa the completely ruined Jina temple of Kalavita at Baṅkāpure.

3. He granted lands, purchased after payment of much gold, to provide for gifts to Jaina sages at the holy place Kapana or Koppal, near Hampi, the capital of Vijayanagar Empire.

4. He caused to be erected a splendid Jina temple, from the base to the pinnacle, the original holy place of Kellanagere, formerly founded by the Gaṅgas, of which by lapse of time only the name remained.

5. He caused to be built five more Jina temples at the same place, viz. Kellangere.

6 He constructed the famous temple of Chaturviṁśati-Tīrthaṅkaras at Śravaṇa-Beḷagoḷa in the year 1159 A.D. King Narasiṁha I gave the name of "*Bhavya-Chūḍāmaṅi-Basti*" to this temple as he was very much impressed by seeing this temple and the King also granted for its upkeep the village Savaneru. The temple is popularly known as "*Bhaṇḍāri-Basti*" since Hulla-Rāja was also 'Bhaṇḍāri' or treasurer of King Narasiṁha I.

Thus this trinity of ministers, Chāmuṇḍa-Rāya, Gaṅga-Rāja and Hulla-Rāja, enriched the old traditions of Śravaṇa-Beḷagoḷa by their valuable and lasting contributions.

CHAPTER-VI

BĀHUBALĪ COLOSSUS OF ŚRAVAṆA-BEḶAGOḶA

1. BĀHUBALĪ'S LIFE AND HIS IMAGE

Śravaṇa-Beḷagoḷa is known all over the world for its colossal image of Bāhubalī or Gommaṭeśvara which is regarded as one of the wonders of the world. This marvellous image was caused to be erected on the Vindhyagiri hill in the year 981 A.D. by Chāmuṇḍa-Rāya. But the legendary accounts say that this magnificent image of Bāhubalī was already there on the hill in a concealed manner and that Chāmuṇḍa-Rāya discovered the image and consecrated it in a proper way. Hence to find out the real facts it is necessary to know the original story of Bāhubalī's life, the traditional account of Bāhubalī's image and the historical evidence about the actual installation of image at Śravaṇa Beḷagoḷa in the last quarter of the 10th century A.D.

Bāhubalī, the first Jaina saint to attain liberation in this '*avasarpiṇī kāla*', i.e., the descending half arc of time, was the son of Lord Ṛshabha, the first Jaina Tīrthaṅkara, who flourished at the dawn of civilization and taught mankind the first lessons of a cultured life. Lord Ṛshabha-deva, the son of Nābhirāja and Marudevī, was a patriarch king of Ayodhyā. Lord Ṛshabha-nātha had many sons, among whom Bharata and Bāhubalī were very prominent. Bharata was the crown-prince and he succeeded his father to the throne of Ayodhyā. By his prowess Bharata became the first universal monarch and due to his profound impact on the country, India came to be known as "*Bhāratavarsha*", i.e., the land of Bharata. Bāhubalī was given the kingdom of 'Aśmaka' from South India which he ruled from its capital seat at Podanapura. In this way after dividing his kingdom among his sons, Lord Rshabhadeva retired to the Himālayas and adopted the Jaina ascetic way of life to teach mankind the path of salvation.

In course of time King Bharata was moved with an intense desire to establish his power as *Chakravartī*', i.e., Emperor. Bharata had in possession a wonderful '*Chakra*', i.e., discus, which could not be withstood by any warrior in fight. With the help of this 'Chakra', Bharata conquered all the countries in the six continents known at that time and returned to his capital Ayodhyā. But the 'Chakra' did not enter the capital. Bharata then took this as a sign that there was still another territory on earth which had not been conquered by him, and, after reflection, came to the conclusion that there was only the kingdom of Aśmaka, ruled by his brother Bāhubalī, which had not been subdued by him. Bharata then declared war on his brother Bāhubalī and with his entire army marched towards Podanapura, where Bāhubalī also had gathered his army and was prepared to meet his brother Bharata on the battle-field. When both the armies were about to attack one another, the ministers of both the brothers stepped forward, prayed to their Lords not to fight and said, "O Lords ! both of you are divine personalities and your bodies are invulnerable. Why should these innocent soldiers be massacred and driven to the jaws of death ? You may kindly decide your superiority by a dual combat". Ultimately the spirit of 'Ahiṁsā', i.e., non-violence, triumphed over 'Hiṁsā', i.e., violence, and both the contending brothers Bharata and Bāhubalī, who were also naturally averse to any form of injury to any life, agreed to decide their question by three methods of rightoeus fight, viz.,

(i) *Dṛishṭi-yuddho*', i.e., looking at each other without winking, (ii) '*Jal-Yuddha*', i.e., throwing water on each other's face, and (iii) '*Malla-yuddha*', i.e., wrestling. In all these three combats Bāhubalī became victorious and his army shouted with applause. Thereupon, Bharata lost his temper and resorted to his all powerful 'Chakra', with which he strove to kill his brother. But even this 'Chakra' could do no harm to Bāhubalī. No doubt Bāhubalī remained unhurt, at least in body, yet in his heart he was surely grieved. Though Emperor Bharata felt humiliated, Bāhubali was not elated in spite of his victory. Bāhubali pitied his brother's aggressive nature and the selfish ways of the world. He asked his brother to take over his kingdom and rule over it, renounced the world forthwith and adopted the life of a naked Jaina ascestic. Bharata made obeisance to Bāhubalī and returned to Ayodhyā. Bāhubalī, as an ascestic, was deeply engaged in meditation and was so much immersed in *Dhyāna*', i.e., self-concentration, that he became absolutely unconscious of the external world. An ant-hill grew up at his feet, and even creepers wound themselves around his legs and hands. Subsequently, Bāhubalī obtained absolute knowledge and became the '*Kevalī*', i.e., the Omniscient. All human beings on the earth, animals and birds gathered around Bāhubalī to pay homage and to hear His teachings. No less a person then Emperor Bharata became one of Bāhubali's ardent devotees. Showing the Right Path to the erring world, Bāhubali became a Perfect Soul and attained '*Nirvāṇa*', i.e., Salvation, on mount Kailāśa. Later, the devotion of Bharata was so intense that he erected a standing colossal image of saint Bāhubalī in his memory at Podanapura. The image was 525 bow-lengths in height. In course of time the region around the image having became infested with innumerable '*Kukkuṭa-sarpas*' (The 'Kukkuṭa-sarpa' is a fowl with a serpant's head and neck. It is the emblem of Goddess Padmāvatī') or cockatrices, the statue came to be known as '*Kukkuṭeśvara*'.

2. TRADITION ABOUT BĀHUBALĪ'S IMAGE

The knowledge of this colossal image of Bāhubalī erected by Emperor Bharata at Podanapura created an intense desire in the mind of devoted Chāmuṇḍa-Rāya to see it. As a result, Chāmuṇḍa-Rāya set out in search of it. But on his way at Śravaṇa-Beḷagoḷa he was informed in a dream that the journey was beyond his power owing to the distance and inaccessibility of the region, and that the same image of Bāhubalī would manifest itself on the larger hill at Śravaṇa-Beḷagoḷa by performing a particular feat. Accordingly, when Chāmuṇḍa-Rāya did the feat, the colossal image of Bāhubalī became visible on the summit of the Vindhyagiri hill at Śravaṇa-Beḷagoḷa.

This traditional account of the discovery of the image is extremely interesting and has been given in detail by some classic works in Sanskrit and Kannaḍa languages like :

1. '*Bhujabali-śataka*' of 1550 A.D. written in Sanskrit by Doḍḍaiyā of Piriyapaṭṭaṇa,
2. '*Bhujabali-charite*' of 1614 A.D. written in Kannaḍa by Pañchabana of Śravaṇa-Beḷagoḷa,
3. '*Munivaṁśābhyudaya*' of about 1680 A.D. written in Kannaḍa poems by Chidānanda-kavi,
4. '*Gommaṭeśvara-charite*' of about 1780 A.D. in Kannaḍa by Ananta-kavi,
5. '*Rājāvali-kathe*' of about 1838 A.D. in Kannaḍa by Devachandra, and
6. '*Sthala-purāna*' of 19th century A.D. in Kannaḍa.

A well-known Kannaḍa poet, Pañchakbana, in his '*Bhujabali-charite*', gives the tradition about the image in detail. It states that Ṛshabha-deva or Ādinātha had two sons, Bharata by his wife Yaśasvatī and Bhujabalī or Bāhubalī by his other wife Sunandā. Bhujabalī married Ichchhādevī and was the ruler of Podanapura. Owing to some misunderstanding there was a battle between the two brothers, in which Bharata was defeated. Bhujabali, however, renounced the kingdom and became an ascetic. Bharata had a golden statue, 525 '*marus*'* in height, of Bhujabalī made and set up. Only the gods worshipped the image, the region having become inaccessible to human beings due to 'Kukkuṭa-Sarpas' which infested it. A Jaina teacher, named, Jinasena, who visited southern Madhurā, gave an account of the image at Podanapura to Kālala-Devī, the mother of Chāmuṇḍa-Rāya, who vowed that she would not taste milk until she saw Gommaṭa or Bhujabalī. Being informed of this by his wife Ajitā-Devī, Chāmuṇḍa-Rāya set out with his mother on his journey to Podanapura. In the course of the journey, he stopped at Śravaṇa-Beḷagoḷa, went up the smaller hill to pay homage to Pārśvanatha of the Chandragupta-Basti and to the foot-prints of Bhadrabāhu, and descended. The same night goddess Padmāvatī and god Brahma appeared to him in a dream and said, "Around the god at Podanapura to a considerable distance 'Kukkuṭa-Sarpas' keep guard and will not allow anyone to approach. It is not therefore possible for

**A 'maru' or 'vyara' is the measure of length equal to the space between the tips of the fingers of either hand when the arms are extended.*

you to see him. Pleased with your devotion, he will, however, manifest himself to you on the summit of the larger hill. Purify yourself and discharge a golden shot from your bow from the smaller hill and the god will instantly become visible". The mother Kālala-Devī, too, had a similar dream. The next morning Chāmuṇḍa-Rāya purified himself and standing on a rock on the smaller hill, facing south, discharged from his bow a golden shot to a boulder on the larger hill. As soon as the shot struck the boulder, the head of Gommaṭa revealed itself. When afterwards the officiating priest placed a diamond chisel on the boulder and struck it with a jewel hammer, the layers of stone fell off and the full image became visible. Then with the help of sculptors Chāmuṇḍa-Rāya caused to be made the 'Pātālā-gamba' with Brahma to the right, the 'Yaksha-gaṁba' with Brahma in front, the upper storey, the 'Tyāgada-pillar' with Brahma, the entrance known as 'Akhaṇḍa-Bagilu' carved out of a single stone, and flights of steps here and there. He then made elaborate arrangements for performing the 'abhisheka' or annointment of Gommaṭa. He also founded a village at the foot of the hill and granted for the god a large number of villages (68 named) of the revenue value of 96,000 'Varahas' and named the village as '*Beḷagoḷa*'. He obtained renown by founding this '*abhinava*', i.e., modern Podanapura.

Similarly, the work "*Bhujabalī-Śataka*" composed in Sanskrit verses by Doḍḍaiya gives the tradition with a little variation. It states that in the city of Madhurā in the Draviḍa country there was a king, named Rājamalla, who encouraged the spread of Jaina tenets, and was the worshipper of Siṁhanandī, belonging to the Deśīya gaṇa. His minister was called Chāmuṇḍa-Rāya. One day, when the king sat with his minister in the royal court, a travelling merchant came there and told them that in the north there was a town called Podanapuri, where there was an image of Bāhubalī, also called Gommaṭa, established by Bharata. Hearing this, the devout Chāmuṇḍa-Rāya resolved to visit the shrine of the image, and going home narrated the tale to his mother Kālikā-Devī, whereupon she also wished to go with him to the sacred spot. Chāmuṇda-Rāja then went to his spiritual preceptor, Ajitasena, who revered Siṁhanandī and made a vow before the latter that he will not drink milk till he sees the image of Bāhubalī. Accompanied by

Ācharya Nemichandra, his mother and numerous soldiers and attendants, Chāmuṇḍa-Rāja started on his pilgrimage and reached the Vindhyagiri in Śravaṇa-Beḷagoḷa. In the night the Jaina Goddess *Kushmāndī* (the Yakshī attendent on Nemināttha, the 22nd Tīrthaṅkara) appeared in a dream to Chāmuṇḍa-Rāja, Ācharya Nemichandra and Kālikā-Devī and told them that it was very difficult to go to Podanapuri but on that very hill there is an image of Bāhubalī, formerly established by Rāvaṇa, which will be visible if the hill be cleft by a golden arrow. According to the dream, on the next morning, Chāmuṇḍa-Rāja stood on the hill with his face towards the south and let loose a golden arrow from his bow. Immediately the mountain was cleft in twain, and an image of Bāhubalī became visible. Chāmuṇḍa-Rāja then established and consecrated the image and granted lands for the worship of this image. When king Rājamalla heard of this affair, he conferred the title of "*Rāya*" on Chāmuṇḍa-Rāja and granted further lands for the regular worship of the image.

Further, the '*Gommaṭeśvaca-Charite*' of Ananta-Kavi tells us that on Chāmuṇḍa-Rāya shooting arrows the image of Gommaṭa revealed itself to him. He got it touched up and improved by sculptors and then had it consecrated.

Moreover, according to "*Sthala-purāna** also, the image of Bāhubalī was already in existence at Śravaṇa-Beḷagoḷa. It states that "Chāmuṇḍa-Rāya. King of Dakshiṇa Madhurā, and the descendant of Jaina Kshettri Paṇḍu, set out with his family, escorted by an army of infantry, cavalry, elephants, and charriots, with a view of visiting the god Gommaṭeśvara (500 '*bilu*' high) at Podana-pura, and the 1254 other gods in the smaller temples scattered throughout the surrounding country. *En route* he came to Śravaṇa-Beḷagoḷa Kshettra' having heard a good deal about the god Gommaṭeśvara (18 '*bilu*' high). He repaired the ruined temples and among other ceremonies had that of sprinkling the god performed. He appointed Siddhācharya as Guru of the *Maṭha*, to conduct the daily, monthly, annual and other processions. He established in the *Maṭha* a *Chattram*

**for English translation of "Sthala-Purana", vide Capt. J.S.F, Mackenzie; "Sravana Belagola", Indian Antiquary, vol. II, May 1873, pp. 129-133.*

where food, medicine, and education were provided for pilgrims...For this purpose certain villages, giving an annual revenue of 1,96,000 pagodas, were made over to the temple."

On the same lines in a Kannaḍa work '*Rājāvali-kathe*', written by Deva-Chandra in 1838 A.D., the old story is repeated, with variations in detail. It states Chāmuṇḍa-Rāya was a feudatory chief of king Rājamalla. His mother learnt from Ādi-purāṇa, when this work was being read to her, that in Podanapura there was an image of Bāhubalī. Thereupon she set out with her son to see this image. But on her way on the hill where Bhadrabāhu Svāmī died, she dreamt one night that Padmāvatī appeared to her and said that there is an image of Bāhubalī on that very hill, covered by stones, which was formerly worshipped by Rāma aod Rāvaṇa and also by the latter's wife Mandodarī. On the next morning an arrow was shot and the image of Bāhubalī became visible.

The Kannaḍa poetic composition "*Munivamśābhyudaya*' of Chidānanda-Kavi written in 1680 A.D., also refers to god Rāma in this connection and furnishes the information that Rāma and Sītā brought the images of Gommṭa and Pārśva from Laṅka and were worshipping them respectively on the larger and the smaller hills of Śravaṇa-Beḷagoḷa. It further states that unable to lift these images up, they left them there and went their way.

Thus, in the legendary accounts of the Jainas, we find that Chāmuṇḍa-Rāya was not the person who caused the image of Bāhubalī to be made, but that there was already an image of Bāhubalī on the hill at Śravaṇa-Beḷagoḷa which he established and consecrated in the proper way. The high priest at Śravaṇa-Beḷagoḷa had also stated, according to these traditions, that "in ancient times, an image of Bāhubalī was at this place, self-formed from earth, under the shape of Gomaṭa Īśvara Svāmī which Rāvaṇa, the monarch of the Rākshasas, worshipped to obtain happiness".

3. INSTALLATION OF BĀHUBALĪ IMAGE

The traditional accounts about the Bāhubalī image maintain that the image was already there on the Vindhyagiri hill at Śravaṇa-Beḷagoḷa from ancient times in a concealed form, that Chāmuṇḍa-Rāya came to know about it through divine suggestion and that Chāmuṇḍa-Rāya merely discovered the image and started its worship. But these legendary contentions cannot be accepted as true, because in the books concerned we find only a collection of traditions handed down from mouth to mouth, with variations arising from such a course. Again, the dates of many works containing these traditions cannot be definitely ascertained. But from their style it can be inferred that they were composed long after the establishment of the Bāhubali image and that they were written in the form of narrating stories of a fictional nature. For example, it is stated that the book '*Rājāvalī-kathe*' is "a compendium of Jaina history, legends and chronology, drawn up early in the present century for Devirammā, a lady of the Mysore royal family, by Devachandra of the Jaina establishment at Maleyur". (vide Lewis Rice : "Inscriptions at Shravana-Belgola" (1889), Introduction, page 3). Similarly, the work '*Sthala-purāṇa*' was intended merely to be a collection of legends and fables. To mention one among many inaccuracies in 'Sthalapurāṇa' we may refer to the statemnet that "Chāmuṇḍa-Rāya was the king of Dakshiṇa Madurā and the descendent of Jaina Kshatri Paṇḍu". The historical fact is that Chāmuṇḍa-Rāya was only the minister and not the King.

It is obvious that in these works Chāmuṇḍa-Rāya has been depicted as merely the discoverer of the image, since the writers of these works desired to ascribe to the image a greater antiquity, causing the image to be considered as an object of deeper veneration.

But this major contention of these traditional accounts that Chāmuṇḍa-Rāya discovered the ancient Bāhubali colossus at Śravaṇa-Beḷagoḷa cannot be accepted as historical truth in the absence of other kinds of evidence of a reliable nature. On the contrary there is ample historical evidence based on inscriptions, literary works and other reliable sources to prove that Chāmuṇḍa-Rāya did not discover but did install the Bāhubals colossus. This historical fact can be seen from the following records :

1. *Inscription No. 234* : This lengthy inscription, dated 1180 A.D., is carved on a stone on the left of the doorway of the Gomaṭeśvara temple and contains a poem of Boppaṇa which categorically states that "Chāmuṇḍa-Rāya resolved to erect such an image himself and with great effort succeeded in getting this statue made and set up."

2. *Inscription No. 254 :* This lengthy inscription, dated 1398 A.D., has been carved on the right pillar in Siddhara-Basti situated outside the enclosure on the Vindhyagiri hill and clearly states that "In that city (i.e. Śravaṇa-Beḷagoḷa), excelling the city of Gods, had Chāmuṇḍa-Rāya, with devotion and effort, auspiciously set up on the mountation, for emancipation, the lord Bhujabalī-Gummaṭa, incomprehensible to performers of sacrifices:"

3. *Inscription No. 175 :* This inscription is dated about 983 A.D., and has been carved on the right side and near the feet of Gommaṭeśvara. This inscription in the Kannaḍa language states that:—

'श्री चामुंडराजं माडिसिदं

i:e., Chāmuṇḍa-Rāya caused (this image) to be made.

4. *Inscription No. 176 :* This inscription, dated about 983 A.D., has been carved below inscription No. 175, is in Tamil language, is the translation of inscription No, 175 and is written in Grantha and Vaṭṭeluṭṭu scripts, It states :—

"श्री चामुंडराजन् सेयूव्वित्तान्"

i.e., Chāmuṇḍa-Rājan caused (this image) to be made.

5. *Inscription No. 177 :* This inscription, dated about 1117 A.D., has been carved below inscriptinn No. 176 and is written in Kannaḍa language. It states :—

'श्री गंगराज सुत्तालयवं माडिसिदं"

i.e., Gaṅga-Rāja caused the enclosure to be made.

6. *Inscription No. 179 :* This inscription is dated about 983 A.D., and has been carved on the left and near the feet of Gommaṭeśvara. This inscription is in Marāṭhī language, is written in the Deva-Nāgarī script and states that:—

"श्री चामुंडराजें करवियलें"

i.e. Chāmuṇḍa-Rāja caused (this image) to be made.

7. *Inscription No. 180 :* This inscription, dated about 1117 A.D., has been carved below the inscription No, 179, is in Marāṭhī language and is written in the Deva-Nāgarī script. It states that :—

"श्री गंगराजे सुत्ताले करवियले"

i.e., Gaṅga-Rāja caused the enclosure to be made.

The inscriptions Nos. 179 and 180 have got great historical and cultural importance since they contain complete sentencesin Marāṭhi language and since they are considered as the oldest inscriptions in Marāṭhi language.

Further, the inscriptions Nos. 179 and 180 written in Marāṭhi language are nothing but the translations of inscriptions Nos. 175 and 177 respectively written in the Kannaḍa script.

8. *Work entitled 'Gommaṭa-sāra'* : The fact that Chāmuṇḍa-Rāya made the image of Bāhubalī by his own efforts has been supported by the well-known work named "*Gommaṭa-sāra Karma-kāṇḍa*', composed by Āchārya Nemichandra, the preceptor and therefore the contemporay of Chāmuṇḍa-Rāya, wherein the verses 968 and 969 state that "Let the aphorisms consisting of the Gommaṭa compendium, the Gommaṭa Jina, on the summit of Gommaṭa Hill and the Dakshiṇa (Southern) Kukkuṭa Jina *constructed* by Gommaṭa-Rāya, be victorious. Let that Gommaṭa by whom the face of the image was *constructed* which was seen...by the gods...and sages, be victorious." It is clear from these verses that the image of Gommaṭeśvara caused the hill on which it was situated to be called Gommaṭa Hill, and that Āchārya Nemichandra uses the words "*vinimmiya*", i.e., "constructed by Chāmuṇḍa-Rāya". Further, it is evident that the image established by Chāmuṇḍa-Rāya came to be called the 'Dakshiṇa, i.e., Southern Kukkuṭa Jina' so as to distinguish it from the image of Bāhubalī which was established by Emperor Bharat in Podanapura and which came to be known as '*Kukkuṭeśvara*', when dragons sprung around it. Moreover, Chāmuṇḍa-Rāya, by having this image constructed, came to be called as Gommaṭa-Rāya.

9. *Story of humbling the pride of Chāmuṇḍa-Rāya* : There is one story connected with the image of Gommaṭeśvara which describes how the pride of Chāmuṇḍa-Rāya for establishing such a huge colossus and for arranging its first annointing ceremony at so vast an expense of money and labour was completely humbled by goddess Padmāvatī in the form of an old women named Gullakāyajī.

From these evidences it can be categorically maintained that it was Chāmuṇḍa-Rāya who had the image of Bāhubalī or Gommaṭa constructed. For such a great act he himself came to be known as Gommṭa-Rāya, which would have been hardly possible, had it been the fact that he merely discovered the image. Āchārya Nemichandra, the preceptor of Chāmuṇḍa-Rāya, must have been present at the time of the establishment of this image (for even in 'Bhujabali charite' it is mentioned that Āchārya Nemichandra was present on this occasion), and consequently the words of Nemichandra, supported as they are by various inscriptions, must be accepted to be conclusive on this point.

Thus it is quite evident that this colossal image of Bāhubalī was carved out of a great rock which stood on the top of the Vindhyagiri hill at Śravaṇa-Beḷagoḷa as otherwise it would have been impossible to transport a granite mass of such huge size up the hill side to the height of 470 feet from the level of the ground below. The *Sthalapurāṇa*', mentions a local legend that Maya, the carpenter of the giants, at Rāvaṇa's request, was the sculptor of this image. (vide 'Indian Antiquary', vol. II, May1873, pp. 129-130). Of course this legned cannot be relied on. But it is stated in the 'Mysore Gazetteer' that among the famous sculptors of South India at that time, viz., Bāligrāma, Charaṇa Haṁpa, Maliyaṇṇa, Nāgoja and Arishṭa Nemī, the image of Bāhubalī was sculptured by Arishṭa Nemi alias Arrito Nemi. People also believe that Arishṭa-Nemi was the sculptor of this image. There is also a popular belief that Arishṭa-Nemi, the sculptor, was a Jaina monk. Any way it appears that one reputed artist Arishṭa-Nemī was the sculptor who executed the work and completed it by 980 A.D. Even though Arishṭa-Nemi actually executed the work of sculpture it may be specifically noted that it was Chāmuṇḍa-Rāya who not only first conceived the idea of having a colossal image of Bāhubalī out of the standing rock on the top of the Vidhyagiri hill at Śravaṇa-Beḷagoḷa but also supplied the details to be shown on and near the image. Obviously in this conception about Bāhubalī's image Chāmuṇḍa-Rāya was greatly influenced by the most vivid and memorable description of Bāhubali given by the great Kannaḍa poet Pampa in his master-piece '*Ādi-purāṇa*', composed in 941 A.D. In this popular work the poet Pampa had painted in words a truely magnificent picture of Bāhubalī. And it was Chāmuṇḍa-Rāya who gave a tangible shape to this word-picture of Bāhubalī and thus made a permanent contribution to world civilization.

4. 'GOMMAṬA' NAME OF THE IMAGE

The image of Bāhubalī installed by Chāmuṇḍa-Rāya became extremely popular by the name 'Gommaṭa' as both the words '*Bāhubalī*' and '*Gommaṭa*' refer to the same person, viz, '*Manmatha*', i.e., cupid, or '*Kāmadeva*'. As according to Jaina scriptures Bāhubalī is the first 'Kāmadeva' of this age, he is also known as 'Manmatha'. This Sanskrit word 'Manmatha' becomes, as per rules of derivation given in the work 'Prākrita-mañjarī' written by Kātyāyana, '*Gammaha*' in Prakrit language and the latter's derivative form in Kannaḍa language becomes '*Gammaṭa*'. The word '*Gammaṭa*' later on became '*Gommaṭa*' in the colloquial form of Kannaḍa language as is clear from similar words like 'Magu' becoming 'Mogu' and 'Sappu' becoming 'Soppu' in the colloquial Kannaḍa.

Further, it is likely that the Kannaḍa word 'Gommaṭa' might have been derived from the word '*Gomaṭo*' or '*Gommaṭo*' in the Koṅkaṇī language meaning 'beautiful'. The word 'Gomaṭo' or 'Gommaṭo' from the Koṅkaṇī language has been used in the Marāṭhi language also in the same sense 'beautiful'. Again, the word 'Gomaṭo' or 'Gommaṭo' has been derived from the Sanskrit word 'Manmatha' meaning cupid. It is, therefore, suggested that the word 'Gommaṭa' in Kannaḍa language might have been adopted from Koṅkaṇi language and through Maraṭhi language since there were very close contacts between the persons belonging to these three languages.

Any way, the word '*Gommaṭa*' is derived from the Sanskrit word '*Manmatha*' and refers to '*Kāmadeva*'. Since Bāhubalī is the first 'Kāmadeva' of this age according to Jaina scriptures, and is also 'Manmatha', he popularly became known as Gommaṭa', or 'Gommaṭa-Jina', or 'Gommaṭeśa', or 'Gommaṭeśvara'. Naturally, the image of Bāhubalī in Karnāṭaka is termed as the image of Gommaṭa, and this term for Bāhubalī has now been adopted by other languages like Marāṭhī, Hindī, etc.

CHAPTER-VII

GOMMAṬEŚVARA IMAGE OF ŚRAVAṆA-BEḶAGOḶA

1. CONSECRATION OF THE IMAGE

From all the available and reliable evidences of a historical nature it is quite clear that the colossal image of Bāhubalī or Gommaṭa was caused to be erected by Chāmuṇḍa-Rāya and that the image was carved out of a great rock which stood on the top of the Vindhyagiri hillat Śravaṇa-Beḷagoḷa. When the entire work of installation of the image was completed the '*Pratishṭhāpanā Mahotsava*', i.e., the Consecration Ceremony, according to strict religious rites, was performed on an auspicious day by Chāmuṇḍa-Rāya on a very large scale and in a manner befitting his extremely high political status and the extra ordinary size and special location of the image at a renowned sacred place of great antiquity and historical significance. But Unfortunately the exact date of the consecration of the image was not known for a long time as it has not been specifically mentioned in any of the innumerable inscriptions found at Śravaṇa-Beḷagoḷa and at other important places in Karnāṭaka. Still continuous efforts were made by various research scholars in the fields of literature, history and archaeology to fix the date of the consecration ceremony on the basis of other kinds of evidence. As a results, different dates were suggested in this connection for acceptance by reputed scholars as follows ;

Date suggested		*Scholar*
Sunday,	10-3-908	Prof. S. Shrikantha Shastri
Sunday,	2-4-980	Shri S.C. Ghoshal
Sunday.	13-3-981	Shri Manjeshvara G. Pai
—	983	B. Lewis Rice and R. Narsimhachar
Sunday,	3-3-1028	Dr. R. Shama Shastri

Out of these scholars, B. Lewis Rice, the Director of Archaeogical Researches in Mysore, was the first to suggest the year 983 A.D., as the year of the consecration of the image in his well-known books, *Inscriptions at Shravana-Belagola,* published in 1889 A.D., and *Inscriptions from Mysore and Coorg* published in 1908 A.D., For a considerable period, this year, i.e., 983 A.D. was treated as the year of consecration. But serious doubts were expressed about the year 983 A.D. and, during the last 50 years, other dates were suggestad. Out of these dates, now the date Sunday, the 13th of March, 981 A.D. has been generally accepted. It is really educative and interesting to know how this date is arrived at.

Chāmuṇḍa-Rāya, the great Jaina warrior, scholar and devotee, served as the prime minister and commander-in-chief under the three famous kings of the Gaṅga dynasty of Taḷakāḍ, viz., (i) Mārasiṁha (961-974 A.D.), (ii) Rājamalla (974-984 A.D.), and (iii) Rakkasa-Gaṅga. It was during this period of service that Chāmuṇḍa-Rāya installed the gigantic colossus of Bāhubalı or Gommaṭa at Śravaṇa-Beḷagoḷa and it was in recgonition of that unmatched and unmatchable pious act of his that the king conferred upon him the title of "Rāya", which means a king or prince, and which finds a modern equivalent in that of "prince" conferred upon Count Bismarck by the German Kaisar. With a view to fixing the date during this period of service, the following facts can be asserted on the basis of the investigation of relevant sources :

(i) *Date not before 974 A.D.* : It is a fact that during the reign of King Mārasiṁha (961-974 A.D.), Chāmuṇḍa-Rāya distinguished himself as a valient warrior, and that in an inscription in which he gives an account of himself he only makes mention of the victories which he had won. There is no mention at all of any religious work done by him, and had it been the fact that he erected the colossal image during the reign of King Mārasiṁha, he would have mentioned the same, it being a mounmental work which has immortalised his name. King Mārasiṁha died in the year 974 A.D. at Baṅkāpura, after having taken a vow of 'Sallekhanā' at the feet of his 'guru', Ajita-Sena, who was also the guru of Chāmuṇḍa-Rāya. It means that the Gommaṭa Image was not consecrated before 974 A.D.

(ii) *Date not before 978 A.D.* : (a) Chāmuṇḍa-Rāya, in his Kannaḍa prose work entitled "*Trishashṭhi-lakshaṇa Mahāpurāṇa*", which he finished on Monday, the 18th of February 978 A.D., refers to almost all his great deeds, whether performed in the service of country or of Dharma, and also enumerates almost all the military and spiritual titles that accrued to him, but still does not utter even a syllable as regards the greater act of his life, viz., the installation of the colossal image of Bāhubalī, which more than any, nay more than all else put together, would surely transmit his name to the remotest posterity. (b) Further, among his many titles that have been mentioned in the above work, that of '*Rāya*', which was conferred upon him by King Rājamalla only on account of, and, therefore, only subsequent to the installation of the colossus, is conspicuous by its absence. It is clear that in all later writings by his protege poet Ranna and by his 'guru' Āchārya Nemichandra, the minister was often called by the name "Rāya". But this title and fond name, viz., "*Rāya*" has not been mentioned in his work "Trishashṭhi-lakshaṇa-Mahāpurāṇa", even though practically all other titles are mentioned. In view of these it can be safely asserted that Chāmuṇḍa-Rāya had not installed the colossus when in 978 A.D. he finished this Kannaḍa work.

(iii) *Date not after 984 A.D.* : In inscription No. 234 at Śravaṇa-Beḷagoḷa, it is specifically stated in clear terms that the colossus was installed by Chāmuṇḍa-Rāya in the reign of King Rājamalla. As the year 984 A.D., is the year of King Rājamalla's death, it means that the colossus was installed before 984 A.D.

Thus putting these three facts together it is clear that the colossus was installed during a period of seven years between 978 A.D. and 984 A.D.

(iv) *Date mentioned in "Bāhubalī Charitra"* : In a Sanskrit poem called "Bāhubalı Charitra" occurs a verses, No. 64 in Canto V, which purports to contain the exact date and moment of this consecration. This verse is as follows :

कल्क्यब्दे षट्शताख्ये विनुत विभवसंवत्सरे मासि चैत्रे
पंचम्यां शुक्लपक्षे दिनमणिदिवसे कुंभलग्ने सुयोगे ।
सौभाग्ये मस्तनाम्नि प्रकटित-भगने सुप्रशस्तां चकार
श्रीमच्चामुंडराजो बेल्गुलनगरे गोमटेशप्रतिष्ठाम् ॥

This verse categorically states that "Chāmuṇḍa-Rāya performed the consecration of Lord Gommaṭa in the city of Beḷaguḷa (i.e. Śravaṇa-Beḷagoḷa).

(ii) in the Kalki year six centuries,
(ii) in the praiseworthy (cyclic) called Vibhava,
(iii) in the month of Chaitra,
(iv) on the fifth lunar day of the bright half (of that month),
(v) on Sunday,
(vi) when the 'Lagna' or zodiacal sign of Kuṁbha (i.e. Aquarius) was in the ascendant,
(vii) with the 'Yoga' called Saubhāgya, and
(viii) the lunar constallation being 'Masta', (i.e., the constallation of 'Mrigashira' or Orion's head".

In the light of this verse the period of seven years between 978 to 984 A.D. was scrutinised and it was found that only in the year 981 A.D. the date of consecration viz., the lunar date of Chaitra Śukla Pañchamı (i.e., the fifth lunar day of the bright half of the lunar month Chaitra) fell on a Sunday as recorded in the verse, that was on Sunday, the 13th of March 981, and that on this day all the other specific astronomical conditions mentioned in the verse were present. On the basis of this scrutiny Shri Manjeshwara Govinda Pai, the great research scholar, finally states as follows : "Thus the facts recounted in this verse lead us to the only conclusion that the great Jaina devotee Chāmuṇḍa-Rāya had the Gommaṭa Colossus installed at Śravaṇa-Beḷagoḷa in the small hours of the night of Sunday, the 13th of March 981 A.D."

Hence the date, the 13th of March, 981 A.D., has now been accepted as the date of '*Pratishṭhā*', i.e., consecration of the Gommaṭeśvara Image and accordingly the 1000th anniversary of its installation is being celebrated on the 22nd of February, 1981 A.D.,

2. CHARACTERISTIC FEATURES OF THE IMAGE

The colossal image of Gommaṭeśvara is a monolithic statue carved out of a living rock on the top of the Vindhyagiri hill at Śravaṇa-Beḷagoḷa as it was quite impossible to transport a granite mass of such huge size up the hill. The image is carved in fine grained light-grey granite.

The height of the image is about 57 feet, and it is an unmistakable landmark for miles around. Such large images sculptured in stone are not uncommon in India, Tibet, Burma and other places outside India, wherever Buddhism and Jainism flourished and wielded their influence. But this image of Gommaṭeśvara happens to be the largest of such images found not only in India but in the entire world and at the same time most beautiful and best preserved since its installation and consecration strictly in accordance with the Jaina rituals one thousand years ago.

The image of Gommaṭeśvara is nude and stands erect facing north. The standing position is according to the '*Kāyotsarga*' or '*Khadgāsana*' posture of practising penance generally prevalent among the Jaina ascetics from ancient times. In this posture the person has to stand erect in a motionless condition with legs nearly touching each other, with both arms fully stretched and invariably kept hanging near the knees, with '*nāsikāgra drishṭi*'. i.e., open eyes looking continuously in the direction of the tip of the nose and with complete engrossment in meditation and self-contemplation. Even a slight deviation in this posture is not permitted irrespective of the severe physical strains involved and of the encroachments and attacks of the living creatures from outside. Naturally the figure of Gommaṭeśvara is treated conventionally, the shoulders being very broad and the arms hanging straight down the sides, with the thumbs turned upwards. The waist is comparatively small and from the knee downwards the legs appear to be somewhat dwarfed.

The face of the image is a remarkable one, with a serene expression. The hair is curled in short spiral ringlets all over the head, while the ears are long and large. This majestic image is most grand and impressive due to its sublime meditative expression. The sculptor, whoever he was, was most skillful in drawing from the blank rock such wonderful contemplative expression touched with a faint winning smile as is seen on the face of the image.

The image has no support above the thighs. Upto that point it is represented as surrounded by ant-hills, from which emerge serpents; and a climbing plant twines itself round both legs and both arms, terminating at the upper part of the arm in a cluster of berries or flowers. According to the Jainas the plant is '*Mādhavī*' (i.e. 'Gaertnera racemosa'), a large creaper with fragrant white flowers, which springs up and blossms in the hot weather. It appears to be known as '*Kaḍu-gulaguñjī*, in Kannaḍa and '*Mādhavī*' in Hindī and Marāṭhī.

The pedestal of the image is designed to represent an open lotus, and upon this the artist worked a scale corresponding to three feet four inches, which was probably used in laying out the work. The outstanding thing about this scale engraved near the left foot of the image is that it corresponds with the French metre. That is why B. Lewis Rice states that "the use of this scale in the tenth century would form an interesting subject for enquiry". This scale is shown divided into equal halves in the middle, where there is a mark resembling a flower. According to some old residents of the place this measure, when multiplied by eighteen, gives the height of the image; but they cannot give any satisfactory reason for multiplying it by eighteen. According to others the measure represents the length of a bow, but the length of a bow is supposed to be three and a half cubits and not three feet four inches.

Owing to the great height of the image and the want of any point sufficiently elevated from which to take a picture of it, most of the representations fail to give a good idea of the features of the face, which are most perfect artistically. The face with its wonderful contemplative expression is touched with a faint smile with which Gommaṭa gazes the struggling world below.

The spirit of Jaina renunciation is fully brought out in this image. The nudity of the image indicates absolute renunciation, while its stiff and erect posture suggests perfect self-control. The smile on the face shows the inward bliss and sympathy for the suffering world. In every sense, the image looks majestic and impressive.

The majesty and the beauty of this great image has kindled

the imagination of many a Kannaḍa poet, of the past and present, to sing praises of it in beautiful poetry. For example, the Jaina poet Boppaṇṇa, also known as Sujanottaṁsa, composed a short Kannaḍa poem in praise of Gommaṭa. This poem has been engraved on a stone to the left of the doorway of the Gommaṭeśvara temple and this inscription No. 234 at Śravaṇa-Beḷagoḷa is dated as 1180 A.D. This poem, inscribed on stone, gives particulars about the life of Gommaṭa and the setting up of the image of Gommaṭa by Chāmuṇḍa-Rāya and then bestows his praise on the image of Gommaṭa thus :

"When an image is very lofty, it may not have beauty; when possessed of loftiness and real beauty, it may not have supernatural power : loftiness, real beauty and mighty supernatural power being all united in it, how worthy of worship in the world is the glorious form, comparable to itself, of Gommaṭeśvara-Jina? When it is said that Maya (the artist of the gods), Indra (though possessed of 1000 eyes) and the lord of serpents (though possessed of 2000 tongues) are unable respectively to draw a likeness, to take a full view and to undertake the praise of it, who else could then be able to do that and to undertake the praise of the matchless form of wonderous beauty of the southern Kukkuṭeśvara? The famous world of the Nāgas always forming the foundation, the earth the base, the points of the compass the walls, the region of heaven the roof, the cars of the gods above the towers, and the cluster of brilliant stars the inner broad jewel-awning, the three worlds enlightened by Jina's sayings have thus become the abode of Gommaṭeśa.

Is he of matchless beauty? He is Cupid.
Is he mighty? He is the conqueror
of the Emperor Bharata.
Is he liberal? He gave back the whole
earth though he had completely
conquered it.
Is he free from attachment? He is
engaged in penance and contents
himself with the two feet of
earth under his two feet.
Is he possessed of perfect knowledge?
He has destroyed the bonds

of 'Karma'.

This said, how exalted is Bāhubalīś ? No man shall take pleasure in killing, lying, stealing, adultery and coveteousness; if he does, he will lose for ever this world and the next: 10: Gommaṭeśvara looks as if proclaiming this standing on high. The anthills and the pressing and entwining creepers on the body looking as if the earth and creeper-like women owing to their grief came and tightly embraced him, saying, "Why have you forsaken us?", the state of Gommaṭadeva's intense application to penance was worthy to be honoured by the lords of serpents, gods and sages."

Like the native poets, the foreigners were also immensely impressed by the characteristic features of the colossal image of Gommaṭa. The foreign travellers, W.H. Workman, and W.J. Workman, record their views in their travelogue, '*Through Town and Jungle*' thus :

"It is probable that Gommaṭa was cut out of the boulder which rested on the spot, as it would have been a work of great difficulty to transport a granite mass of this size up the oval hillside. It is larger than any of the statues of Rameses in Egypt.

The figure is standing with shoulders squared and arms hanging straight. Its upper half projects above the surrounding ramparts. It is carved in a fine-grained light-grey granite, has not been injured by weather or violence, and looks as bright and clean as if just from the chisel of the artist.

Gommaṭeśwara has watched over India for only 1000 years, whilst the statues of Rameses in Egypt have gazed the Nile for more than 4000 years. The monolithic Indian saint is thousands of years younger than the prostrate Rameses or the guardians of Abu Simbal, but he is more impressive, both on account of his commanding position on the brow of the hill overlooking the wide stretch of plain and of his size."

Similarly, the famous art historian of India, J. Fergusson, in his celebrated work '*History of Indian and Eastern Architecture*,' describes the excellence of this image in the world thus :

"The statue is the most remarkable work of native art in the south of India. This statue attracted the attention of the late Duke of Wellington when, as Sir Arthur Wellesley, he commanded a division at the siege of Seringapatam. He, like all those who followed him, was astonished at the amount of labour such a work must have entailed, and puzzled to know whether it was a part of the hill or had been moved to the spot where it now stands. The former is the more probable theory. The hill is one mass of granite about 400 feet in height, and probably had a mass or Tor standing on its summit—either a part of the adjacent mass or lying on it. This the Jains undertook to fashion into a statue of 58 feet in height, and hence achieved it with marvellous success...Whether, however, the rock was found *'in situ'* or was moved, nothing grander or more imposing exists anywhere out of Egypt, and even there no known statue surpasses it in height."

3. DIMENSIONS OF THE IMAGE

There had been a great curiosity to know the exact dimensions of the colossal image of Gommaṭeśvara. Different estimates of the height of the image of Gommaṭa were given : 70 feet 3 inches by Buchanan and 60 feet 3 inches by Sir Arthur Wellesley. But Mr. Bowing, the then Chief Commissioner of Mysore, put the hight as 57 feet by actual measurement and in his book "*Eastern Experiences*" he said that "The colossal statue was measured by my order on the Ist of January 1865 and the height then assigned was 57 feet. The measurement was made by the Amildar. A platform was specially erected to ascertain the exact height of the statue, which was found to be 57 feet, and not 70 feet, as generally supposed."

Later, a serious attempt was made to take the measurements of the different parts of the image by Mr. Scandon, the officer of the Public Works Department in 1871 at the time of the great head-annointing ceremony of the image for which a large platform was specially erected. Unfortunately, before Mr. Scandon could complete the work, some of the priests interfered. Still this was the first and only time when some detailed measurements were taken. These measurements are considered as correct and have been given by Capt. J.S F. Mackenize of Mysore in his article on "Śravaṇa-Beḷagoḷa" (vide "Indian Antiquary", vol. II, May 1873). The following were the dimensions obtained :

		Feet	Inches
1.	Total height to the bottom of the ear	—	50-0
2.	From the Bottom of the ear to the crown of the head (not measured), about	—	6-6
3.	Length of the foot	—	9-0
4.	Breadth across the front of the foot	—	4-6
5.	Length of the great toe	—	2-9
6.	Half girth at the instep	—	6-4
7.	Half girth of the thigh	—	10-0
8.	From the hip to the ear	—	24-6
9.	From the coccyx to the ear	—	20-0
10.	Breadth across the pelvis	—	13-0
11.	Breadth at the waist	—	10-0
12.	From the waist and elbow to the ear	—	17-0
13.	From the armpit to the ear	—	7-0
14.	Breadth across the shoulders	—	26-0
15.	From the base of the neck to the ear	—	2-6
16.	Length of the forefinger	—	3-6
17.	Length of the middle finger	—	5-3
18.	Length of the third finger	—	4-7
19.	Length of the fourth finger	—	2-8

These measurements appear to be fairly correct and have been accepted. The height of the statue has been put down at 57 feet.

Further, in the private library of Mr. Aramane Jina-Chandraiyā of Mysore there is a palm-leaf manuscript which contains 16 Sanskrit stanzas composed by a Jaina poet of the name of Śāntarāja-paṇḍita, who also bore the title of 'Kavi-chakravartī', i.e., emperor of poets. In the last stanza it is mentioned that the poet himself took the measurements of the image by order of his patron, the Mysore King Krishṇa-Rāja-Oḍeyār III, on the occasion of the anointment of the god caused to be performed by that king. The poet has given the measurements of the different parts of the image in '*hastas*' (i.e. cubits) and '*angulas*' (i.e. finger-breadths). The poet also states that the measurements are given for the pious contemplation of his co-religionists and for the astonishment of the adherents of other religions. In these stanzas other names of Gommaṭa, viz., Dorbalī, Bāhubalī and Saunandī (i.e. son of Sunandā) are used. There seems to be some mistake in stanza 14. The following measurements are given in these stanzas :

	'Hastas' 'Anqulas'
1. From the foot to the crown of the head.	36.1/8-0
2. From the foot to the navel	20-0
3. From the navel to the head	16.1/8-0
4. From the chin to the crown of the head	6-3
5. Length of the ear	2.3/4-0
6. From ear to ear	8-0
7. Girth of the neck	10.3/4-0
8. Height of the neck	1.3/4-0
9. From shoulder to shoulder	16-0
10. The lines around the nipple	4-9
11. Girth of the waist	20-0
12. From the shoulder to the middle finger	18½-0
13. Girth of the wrist	6½-0
14. Length of the thumb	2.1/4-0
15. Length of the great toe	4½
16. Length of the foot	4-1

According to the poet the height of the image is 54 feet and 3 inches. He also gives the dimensions of several parts not given in the previous list.

4. INSPIRATION TO SIMILAR IMAGES

The installation of the colossal image of Gommaṭeśvara on the Vindhyagiri hill at Śravaṇa-Beḷagoḷa on Sunday, the 13th of March, 981 A.D. by Chāmuṇḍa-Rāya proved to be an event of great historical significance from the point of view of the position of Jainism in Karnāṭaka. This memorable event created a deep impact on the minds of the people in general and of the Jainas in particular. The installation of this most lofty and and at the same time most beautiful image, which was without a parallel in the history of Karnāṭaka at that time, not only raised the prestige of the Jainas among the general people of Karnāṭaka but also provided sufficient inspiration for the Jaina chieftains and rulers of different dynasties in Karnāṭaka to emulate the noble example of Chief Minister and Military General Chāmuṇḍa-Rāya by erecting similar colossal images of Bāhubalī on the tops of the hills in their regions. Accordingly, three colossal images of Bāhubalī were set up at (i) Kārkala (Distt. South Kanara), (ii) Veṇūra (Dist. South Kanara) and (iii) Gommaṭagiri (Dist. Mysore) in Karnāṭaka upto the 17th century A.D. and at (iv) place called Bāhubalī (Dist. Kolhāpur) in Mahārāshṭra and (v) Dharmasthala (Dist. South Kanara) in the 20th century A.D.

(1) *Bāhubalī Colossus at Kārkala :* The rulers of Kārkala in the 15th century were warm supporters of Jaina religion and the credit of making them the followers of the Jaina doctrine goes to the Jaina 'gurus' of Hanasoge. It was at the instance of Lalitakīrtī Maladhārīdeva Bhaṭṭāraka of Hanasoge that chieftain Vīra Paṇḍya, the son of Bhairavendra, caused to be constructed and set up the colossal image of Gommaṭa on the top of a hill at Kārkala on Wednesday, the 13th of February, 1432 A.D.. The image is 41 feet 5 inches high, 10⅓ feet broad, 10 feet thick and weighing about 80 tons. This huge image was carved from the block which was cut and taken from the southern slope of the hill and after transporting it was erected on the hill about 300 feet high at Kārkala. The question naturally arises as to how this huge image was moved to its place. In this connection Fergusson, the art historian of India, says; " The task of carving a rock standing in its place had it even been twice the size, the Hindu mind never would have shrunk from; but to move such a mass up the steep smooth side of the hill seems a labour beyond their power, even with all their skill in concentrating masses of men on a single point." Yet the fact remains that, at least at kārkala, the statue with its immense proportions was moved up a smooth and steep rock nearly 300 feet high. According to tradition (—mentioned by E. Thurstone in his book. '*The Castes and Tribes of Southern India*,' vol, II. PP. 422-23), the statue was raised on to a train of twenty iron carts furnished with steel wheels, on each of which 10,000 propitiatory coconuts were broken, and covered with an infinity of cotton, it was then drawn, by legions of worshippers up an inclined plane to the platform on the hill-top, where it now stands.

About this image of Bāhubalī at Kārkala, Walhouse, the famous art critic says that "This is one of those colossal statues that are found in this part of the country, statues truly Egyptian in size, and unrivalled throughout India as detached works...Nude, cut from a single mass of granite, darkened by the monsoons of centuries, the vast statue stands upright, with arms having straight, but not awkwardly, down the sides in a posture of somewhat stiff but simple dignity."

(ii) *Bāhubalī Colossus at Veṇūra :* Timmarāja, the ruler of Puñjalike Rājya, who claims descent from the family of famous Chāmuṇḍa-Rāya who had set up the colossal image at Śravaṇa-Beḷagoḷa. installed at the instance of Chārukīrtī Bhaṭṭāraka of Śravaṇa-Beḷagoḷa the image of Bāhubalī on the top of a hill near the bank of river Phālgunī at Veṇūra in District South Kanara. The colossal image, 35 feet high, was installed on Thursday, the Ist of March, 1604 A.D.

The three colossal monolithic nude Jaina statues at Śravaṇa-Beḷagoḷa, Kārkala and Veṇūra are considered as among the wonders of the world. (vide 'Imperial Gazetteer of India page 121). About the outstanding features of these three images, Dr. Vincent Śmith, the renowned art historian, says thus, "These are undoubtedly the most remarkable of the Jain statues and the largest free-standing statues in Asia...All three being set on the top of eminences, are visible for miles around, and, in spite of their formalism, command respectful attention by their enormous mass and expression of dignified serenity. The biggest, that at Śravaṇa-Beḷagoḷa, stands about 56 feet in height, with a width of 13 feet across the hips, and is cut out of a solid block of gneiss, apparently wrought *in situ.* That at Kārkala, of the same material, but some 15 feet less in height, is estimated to weight 80 tons. The smallest of the giants, that at Veṇūr, is 35 feet high. The three images are almost identical, but the one at Veṇūr has the 'special peculiarity of the cheeks being dimpled, with a deep grave smile', which is considered to detract from the impressive effect. The extreme conventionalism of Jain art is well illustrated by the fact that, whereas all the three colossi are substantially identical, save for the smile at Veṇūr, the dates vary widely". (vide *A History of Fine Art in India and Ceylon*, page 268).

(iii) *Bāhubalī Colossus at Gommaṭagiri :* The 18 feet high image of Bāhubalī has recently been located on the top of a small hill of about 100 feet in height, at Gommaṭagiri, a place in the interior quiet region at about 25 km. distance in the North-West direction from Mysore city on the Mysore-Hunsur Road. Nothing is so far known either about the date or the name of the person at whose instance the statue at this place was erected. It is suggested that the image might have been installed in the 14th century A.D. But it got the public attention only from 1950 A.D. onwards. The third 'Mahāmastakābhisheka', i.e., great head-anointing ceremony, of the image was performed on the 7th of September, 1952 A.D. in the presence of the Rāja-Pramukha of Mysore.

(iv) *Bāhubalī Colossus at Bāhubalī hill* : After a lapse of nearly four centuries, the practice of erecting colossal images of Bāhubalī is gaining ground and is becoming popular not only in Karnāṭaka but in the Mahārāshṭra region adjacent to Karnāṭaka. Accordingly at the sacred place of Bāhubalī hill, also known as Kumbhojagiri, in the Hātakaṇangale Talukā of Kolhāpur District (Mahārāshṭra State) situated at about 20 kilometers from Kolhāpur city, the 28 feet high colossal image of Gommaṭeśvara was consecrated on the 8th of February, 1963. The peculiarity of this image is that while other colossal images of Bāhubalī are carved out of granite stone, this image at Bāhubalī hill has been carved out of white shining marble. This huge image was carved near the marble quarry in Rājasthān and was transported to the Bāhubalī hill by rail and road after making specially deigned carriages which were drawn on sandy and soft roads covered with thick metal sheets. In addition, the pedestal of the image is carved out of pink marble and is designed to represent an open lotus. On the pedestal of this image two artistic pink marble statues in the sitting posture of Chāmuṇḍa-Rāya, the pioneer of erecting colossal Gommaṭa statues, and of Gomatī-Devī alias Gullakāyajī, the legendary devoted old woman, have been placed on the left and right side of the image respectively. Such statues of these two prominent devotees are not found elsewhere. Again this image has been installed at the instance of the great Jaina Āchārya Chāritra-chakravartī Śanti-sāgara Mahāraj. Further, this image has been installed not by any single person but by a Jaina educational institution, known as Bāhubalī Brahmacharyāśrama, (—the pioneer institution of Jaina Gurukula system of education) under the guidence of its founder saint Gurudeva

Samanta-bhadra Mahāraj. Further more, this image has been installed not on the top of the hill but at a height of 50 feet on the slope of the hill and is surrounded by the replicas, made by concrete and stone, of the prominent sacred places in India. The outstanding feature of this image is that it has been installed at the place which is the centre of nearly three lakhs Jaina population-especially rural Jaina population and in the area which has got the highest density of Jaina population in India. Such concentration of Jaina population is not found at other places where colossal Gommaṭa images have been erected. Moreover, this image has revived the practice of erecting colossal images of Bhuābalī after a long interval of 360 years, since it is the first statue of this type to be erected after the statue of Bāhubalī erected in 1604 A.D. at Veṇūra in South Kanara. This example is being followed by others.

(v) *Bāhubalī colossus at Dharma-Sthala :* Shri D. Vīrendra Heggaḍe, the Jaina '*Dharmādhikārī*', i.e., the traditional administrative head, of the Hindu sacred place Dharmsthala in South Kanara District has caused to be made monolithic stone statue 52 feet high weighing about 210 tons. This colossal statue of Bāhubalī was carved at Kārkala by the famous old sculptor Shri Renjal Gopal Shenoy. This gigantic statue, which is next in height to that of the statue of Gommaṭeśvara at Śravaṇa-Beḷagoḷa was transported from Kārkaḷa to Dharmāsthala and was ceremoniously received on the 23rd of March, 1973 A.D. at the hill known as Shri Bāhubalī Vihār in Dharmāsthala town, This impressive image of Bāhubalī has been erected at the place Shri Bāhubalī Vihār and it is planned to organise the "consecration ceremony" of the image in 1982 A.D.

Thus at present there are six similar colossal images of Bāhubalī in South India as follows :

Sr. No.	*Date of consecration*	*Place*	*Height feet*	*Quality of stone*
1.	13-3-981	Śravaṇa-Beḷagoḷa	57	Light-grey granite
2.	13-2-1432	Kārkala	41′.5″	Light-deep granite
3.	1-3-1604	Veṇūra	35	Deep-granite
4.	Not known	Gommaṭagiri	18	Black granite
5.	8-2-1963	Bāhubalī Hill	28	White marble
6.	Proposed 1982	Dharmasthala	52	Light-deep granite

(N.B. : These images are shown on the map attached).

In recent times the practice of erecting colossal Bāhubali images is being adopted in North India and accordingly one such image carved in granite at Kārkaḷa in South India has been installed at Ferozabad in Uttara Pradesh. It means that the practice is now becoming popular.

CHAPTER VIII

GRAND FESTIVAL OF ŚRAVAṆA-BEḶAGOLA

1. 'MAHĀMASTAKĀBHISHEKA' CEREMONY

The great general Chāmuṇḍa-Rāya not only installed the colossal image of Gommaṭeśvara on the top of the Vindhyagiri hill at Śravaṇa-Beḷagoḷa but also performed the "*Pratishṭhāpanā Mahotsava*", i.e., the great ceremony of consecration of the image, on Sunday, the 13th of March, 981 A.D. in accordance with the detailed rituals prescribed in Jaina scriptures for the purpose and on a very grand scale befitting both the huge size of the image and the extremely high status of the "*Yajamāna*", i.e., the host. As a part of the sacred ritual the cremony of "*Pañchāmritābhisheka*", i.e., bathing of the image with five liquids, viz, milk, curds, ghee or clarified butter, saffron and water, which is also known as "*Mastakābhisheka*", i.e., the head-anointing ceremony, was performed with grandeur. dignity and solemnity in keeping with the extra-ordinary nature of the occasion. Later on this festival of performing '*Mastakābhisheka*' was continued and it came to be termed as *Mahāmastakābhisheka*" i.e.. the great head-anointing ceremony, since it came to be performed only at certain conjunctions of the heavenly bodies at intervals of several years usually 10 to 15 years, and at a great cost. The huge proportions of the graceful colossus, whose head is anointed on the particular day after an interval of 10 to 15 years by thousands of priests and pilgrims, gives to the ritual an impressive character. Hence the "*Mahāmastakābhisheka*" ceremony is popularly known as the "Grand Festival of Śravaṇa-Beḷagoḷa"

This festival begins about a fortnight earlier and terminates after a fortnight of the 'Mahāmastakābhisheka'. Between these two dates there are various festivals and 'pūjās', i.e., worships. Generally more than two-hundred-thousand pilgrims of Jain religion and thousands of tourists of other religions gather at the village of Śravaṇa-Beḷagoḷa to participate and to witness the 'Mahāmastākabhisheka' ceremony. Since all the participants and the spectators are in the festive religious mood and in their holiday attire, the entire festival becomes a colourful spectacle.

On the morning of the 'Mahāmastakābhisheka' day, the court-yard before the colossus is strewn with layers of fresh paddy. On this green carpet, one thousand-and-eight coloured 'Kalaśas' i.e., pots filled with sacred water are arranged in rows, sticking out from the mouth of each, a coconut with ceremonial dressing of mango leaves fastened with coloured sacred twine. Out of these 1008 pots, 900 pots are used for the first anointing, 103 pots for the second, and only 5 pots for the third and last anointing.

When ceremony is due to start, a number of Jaina priests take up their positions on the high scaffoldings specially prepared out of strong wooden pillars for the purpose. Each priest holds in his hands one 'Kalaśa', i.e., a pot brimming over with milk, and one pot with ghee. At a signal of the officiating dignitory, they start the anointing or bath by pouring potfuls of milk over the image. Then ghee follows.

After these preliminary baths or anointings, Gommaṭeśvara is worshipped till noon by the Jaina priests. At the stroke of 1 o'clock, the great 'Mahāmastakābhisheka' begins. The former Mahārājas of Mysore State had always been the greatest patrons of this colossal image of Gommaṭeśvara, since its installation at Śravaṇa-Beḷagoḷa, a part of their Kingdom, and it is they who had the hereditary privilege of performing the first 'pūjā' or worship of the image on this auspicious occasion.

As the appointed hour draws near, the thousand priests climb to their places on the scaffolding with pots of water. Suitable music is played by temple musicians while the priests chant hymns and prayers from Jaina sacred texts. Meanwhile the vast assembly of the pilgrims shout orations in praise of Gommaṭeśvara. Then at the bidding of the Master of the Ceremony, the thousand pots of water are emptied over the image.

Following these baths 15 other offerings are showered on Gommaṭeśvaṛa image in the following order :

1. Water	2. Cocoanut	3. Plantains
4. Jaggery	5. Ghee	6. Sugar
7. Almonds	8. Dates	9. Poppy-seeds
10. Milk	11. Curds	12. Sandal
13. Gold flowers	14. Silver flowers	15. Silver coins.

This kind of 'Mahāmastakābhisheka' ceremony was performed on the occasion of the Consecration of the Image on Sunday, the 13th of March, 981 A.D. by General Chāmuṇḍa-Rāya, who was the 'Yajamāna', i.e.., the host, of the grand ceremony as he had caused that image to be installed at great cost. In connection with this first 'Mahāmastakābhisheka' ceremony performed on a very grand scale by Chamuṇḍa-Rāya, there is a legend which describes how the pride of Chāmuṇḍa-Rāya, for installing such a huge image was humbled by a devoted old lady named 'Gullakāyaji'. The story is as follows :

Chāmuṇḍa-Rāya, after having established the worship of this image, became proud and elated, at placing this God by his own authority at so vast an expense of money and labour. Soon after this, when he performed in honour of the God the ceremony of 'Pañchāmritābhisheka', i.e., bathing the image with five liquids, vast quantities of these things were expended in many hundred pots; but, through the wonderful power of the God, the liquid descended not lower than the navel, to check the pride and vanity of the worshipper. Chāmuṇḍa-Rāya, not knowing the cause, was filled with grief that his intention was frustrated of bathing the image completely with this ablution. While he was in this situation, the celestial nymph 'Padmāvatī', by order of the God, having transformed herself into the likeness of an aged poor woman, appeared, holding in her hand the five 'amṛitas', i.e., liquids, in a 'Beḷiya Goḷa' (or small silver pot) for bathing the statue; and signified her intention to Chāmuṇḍa-Rāya, who laughed at the absurdity of this proposal, of accomplishing what had not been in his power to effect. Out of curiosity, however, he permitted her to attempt it, when, to the great surprise of the beholders, she bathed the image with the liquid brought in the little silver vase. Chāmuṇḍa-Rāya, repenting his sinful arrogance, performed a second time, with profound respect, his ablution, on which they formerly wasted so much valuable liquids, and bathed completely the body of the image. From that time this place is named after the 'Beḷiya Goḷa', i.e., the silver vase, which was held in Padmāvatī's hand. (vide 'Asiatic Researches', vol. IX, page 266).

2. CEREMONIES TO THE END OF THE 19TH CENTURY

Written records are available to establish the 'Mahāmastakābhisheka' ceremonies having taken place in the following years upto the end of the 19th century :

1. *In 1398 A.D.* : The earliest reference to 'Mahāmastakābhisheka' is found in inscription No. 254 dated 1398 A.D. which also states that one Paṇḍitārya did perform seven 'Mahāmastakābhishekas' like this prior to it.

2. *In 1612 A.D.* : The poet Pañchabana refers to an anointment caused to be performed by one Śānti Varṇī in the year 1612 A.D.

3. *In 1659 A.D.* : Performed by His Highness Shri Mahārāja Doḍḍa Devarāja Woḍeyār Bahādur of Mysore.

4. *In 1677 A.D.* : Poet Anantakavi refers to the anointment ceremony conducted at the expense of Viśālāksha-Paṇḍita, the Jaina minister of the Mysore King Chikka Devaraja Woḍeyār in 1677 A.D

5. *In 1800 A.D.* : Performed by His Highness the Mahārāja Mummadi Krishṇa-Rāja Woḍeyār (III) Bahādur of Mysore.

6 *In 1825 A.D.* : Mentioned by Paṇḍita Śānti-rāja of its being performed by the Mysore King Krishṇa-Rāja Woḍeyār (III) in about 1825 A.D.

7 *In 1827 A.D.* : In inscription No.223, a specific reference has been made to a similar ceremony performed in 1827 A.D.

8. *In 1871 A.D.* : Capt. J.S.F. Mackenzie of Mysore Commission mentions that "Once in twenty years the great ceremony of washing the god is performed. The last occasion was in the early part of June 1871. (vide 'Indian Antiquary', Vol. II, May 1873, page 129).

9. *In 1887 A.D.* : Śrī Laxmī-Sena Bhaṭṭāraka Swāmī of Kolhāpur Maṭha performed the 'Mahāmastakābhisheka' on the 14th of March 1887 A.D. It is said that this Laxmī-Sena Bhaṭṭāraka spent Rs. 30,000 for this purpose. The following account of the ceremony is taken from the May 1887 issue of

the journal 'Harvest Field' :

"The 14th of March 1887 was the day of anointing for the statue of Gommaṭeśvara. It was a great day in anticipation of which 20,000 pilgrims gathered there from all parts of India. There were Bengalis, there were Gujaratis and there were Tamil people in great numbers. Some arrived a full month before the time and the stream continued to flow until the afternoon of the day of the great festival. For a whole month there was daily worship in all the temples, and 'pāda-pūjā' or worship of the feet of the great idol besides. On the great day, the 14th of March 1887, people began to ascend the hill even before dawn in the hope of securing good places from which to see everything. Among them were large numbers of women and girls in very bright attire, carrying with them brass or earthen pots. By 10 o'clock all available space in the temple enclosure was filled. Opposite the idol an area of 40 square feet was streamed with bright yellow paddy, on which were placed 1,000 gaily painted earthenware pots, filled with sacred water, covered with cocoanuts and adorned with mango leaves. Above the image was a scaffolding, on which stood several priests, each having at hand pots filled with milk, ghee and such like things. At a signal from the Kolhāpur Swāmī, the master of the ceremonies, the contents of these vessels were poured simultaneously over the head of the idol. This was a sort of preliminary bath, but the grand bath took place at 2 o'clock. Amid the great dissonance of many instruments the thousand pots already mentioned were lifted as if by magic from the reserved area to the scaffolding and all their contents poured over the image, the priests meanwhile chanting texts from the sacred books. Evidently the people were much impressed. There were mingled cries of "Jai Jai Mahārāja" and 'Ahāhā, 'ahāhā', the distinctive exclamations of Northern and Southern Indians to mark their wonder and approval. In the final anointing fifteen different substances were used, namely : (1) water, (2) cocoanut meal, (3) plantains, (4) jaggery, (5) ghee, (6) sugar, (7) almonds, (8) date, (9) poppy seeds, (10) milk, (11) curds, (12) sandal, (13) gold flowers, (14) silver flowers, and (15) silver coins. With the gold and silver flowers there were mixed nine varieties of precious gems, and silver coins to the amount of Rs. 500/- completed the offering".

10. *In 1900 A.D. :* There is a reference in the 'Indian Antiquary' to the effect that in 1900 A.D. the 'Mahāmastakābhisheka' ceremony was performed.

3. CEREMONIES IN THE 20TH CENTURY

In the present twentieth century the 'Mahāmastakābhisheka' ceremonies ware held on the following days :

(1) the 30th of March 1910,
(2) the 15th of March 1925,
(3) the 26th of February 1940,
(4) the 5th of March 1953, and
(5) the 30th of March 1967,

The iast 'Mahāmastakābhisheka' ceremony has been held on the 22nd of February1981 A.D. It would be worth while to note the important features of these six ceromonies.

1. *On the 30th of March 1910 A.D. :* There was a grand head anointing ceremony on the 30th of March 1910 A.D. On this occasion an interesting event took place, that is, an aerial post was tried by one Mr. G.F. Edwards who sent a message regarding the 'pūjā' i.e. worship, by a homing pigeon which was received by the 'Madras Mail' Newspaper office at Madras within three hours and forty minutes.

His Highness Krishṇa-Rājendra Woḍeyār, the King of Mysore, attended the ceremony and also performed the 'pūjā' of Gommaṭeśvara.

This 'Mahāmastakābhisheka' ceremony proved a great success from the social point of view. On this occasion for the first time a special session of the All-India Digambara Jaina Mahāsabhā was held on a large scale and through the various resolutions passed a definite and new direction to social reforms was given to the society. Among these resolutions the most important was about the scheme sponsored by the enlightened leader and great philanthropist Seth Manikchand Hirachand Zaveri, J.P. of Bombay and his 'guru' Brahmachari Śhitalaprasadaji regarding the imparting of religious education along with the Western or English education to Jaina students and for this specific purpose establishing Jaina Boarding schools at various Jaina centres in India. Accordingly new Jaina Boarding schools were opened at Ahmedabad, Allahabad, Meerut, Belgaum, Sangli, Poona and other important places in India and a new era in education among the Jainas was ushered in. Such Jaina Boarding schools were already established at Bombay, Sholapur, Surat, Kolhapur and Hubli.

2. On the 15th of March 1925 A.D. : After the lapse of a decade and a half, a very grand 'Mahāmastakābhisheka' was performed on the 15th of March 1925 A.D. Months before this date a 'Pūjā Committee' was formed with his Holiness Chārukīrti Bhaṭṭāraka of Jaina Maṭha at Śravaṇa-Beḷagoḷa as the President and Mr. M.L. Vardhamaniah of Mysore as the Secretary. On this occasion Mr. Vardhamaniah initiated a new policy of propaganda for involving large number of Jainas in the festival and accordingly he toured all over India and invited all ranks of Jainas to participate in the festival. As a result, an intense attraction was created, for the first time among the common people to undertake a pilgrimage to Śravaṇa-Beḷagoḷa on this occasion.

The great festival began on the 27th of February 1925 A.D. with different preliminary ceremonies and culminated in the grand 'Mahāmastakābhisheka' ceremony on the 15th March 1925 A.D. Approximately 30,000 people were present for this grand ceremony. His Highness Krishṇa-Rājendra Woḍeyār, the Mahārāja of Mysore, walked up the hill bare-footed, witnessed the entire anointment ceremony, personally performed the 'pūjā', offered 'Śāshṭāṅga-Namaskāra' to Gommateśa image, gave personal donations of Rs. 5000/- to the 'Abhisheka Fund' and Rs. 500/- to the Jaina Maṭha, and showed personal regard by offering 'namaskāra' to His Holiness Chārukīrti Bhaṭṭāraka, the head pontiff of Śravaṇa-Beḷagoḷa.

The most remarkable event of this grand festival was the memorable speech delivered by His Highness Krishṇa-Rājendra-Woḍeyār, the Mahārajā of Mysore, as the President of the All-India Digambara Jaina Conference on the 14th of March 1925. On this occasion an address was presented on behalf of the Jaina community in India to His Highness Krishṇa-Rājendra-Woḍeyār by Shri M.R. Vardhamaniah under the presidentship of Sir Sarupachandaji Hukumachandaji of Indore. While welcoming the Jaina community at large to the land of Mysore symbolising Gommaṭa's spiritual empire, the Mahārajā paid a warm tribute to the past Jaina poets and pandits who made a singular contribution to Kannaḍa literature in its initial stages. The entire speech of the Mahārajā was saturated with a sense of high gratitude to the selfless services of Jaina authors which stand unparalleled in the history of Jainas and Jainism in India. The speech was full of love for Jainism, Śravaṇa-Beḷagoḷa, and Jaina community alike. To quote from the speech of the Mahārajā :

"It gives me great pleasure to be with you on a solemn and auspicious occasion like the present when you have assembled in such large numbers from all parts of India for a holy purpose.

"In welcoming this All-India gathering of the Jainas to the land of Mysore, I cannot forget that this land to them is a land of pilgrimage, consecrated by some of the holiest traditions and tenderest memories of their faith. This picturesque rock on an elevated tableland was, as a thousand years' old tradition has it, the scene where the venerable Bhagwan Shrutakevali Bhadrabahu leading the first migration of the Jainas to the Southern Peninsula broke his journey and took up his abode, and tradition still points to the cave in which he passed away in Sallekhanā. It was in this holy land, the Dakshiṇa Kāshī, the Benaras of the South, that, as the same tradition has it, the Mauryan Emperor Chandragupta, the fame of whose prowess turned away the invincible hosts of Alexander the Great, doffing the Emperor's for the ascetic's robe, nursed his master, the Shrutakevali, in his last moments and worshipped his footprints. Since that day, many a royal prince of the South and many a holy monk of the North have vowed themselves to death by the rite of sallekhanā.

"This is also the holy spot sacred to the Muniśvara Gommaṭa whom tradition represents to have been the younger brother of Bharata, the eponymous Emperor of Bhāratavarsha. The land of Mysore, therefore, symbolises Gommaṭa's spiritual Empire, as Bhāratavarsha stands for the empire of his brother Bharata. For a thousand years the Munishvara's colossal statue carved, as it may be, out of a huge boulder on the rock and visible for miles around has ruled over this scene unsurpassed in massive grandeur and sublimity of spiritual power by anything that the Egyptian or Assyrian monuments can show.

"But Jainism not only found a second birth place and home

in Mysore, it also repaid the debt. For the noblest masterpieces of Kannada literature in its early history have mostly been inspired by Jainism and created by Jainā-chārya and scholars and Jaina learned men have ever since continued to render signal service to it.

"No less memorable have been the services of Jainism to the evolution of India's spiritual and philosophical life. Jainism has cultivated certain aspects of that life which have broadened India's religious outlook. It is not merely that Jainism has aimed at carrying Ahiṁsā to its logical conclusion undeterred by the practicalities of the world, it is not only that Jainism has attempted to perfect the doctrine of the spiritual conquest of matter in its doctrine of the Jina, what is unique in Jainism among Indian religions and philosophical systems is that it has sought Emancipation in an upward movement of the spirit towards the realm of Infinite and Transcendance,—and that it has made Power, Will, Character, in one word Chāritra, an integral element of Perfection side by side with Knowledge and Faith. And Jainism has sought a harmony of all religions and of all philosophical and dialectical standpoints in its Sarvadharma samabhava and Anekāntavāda. At the other end of the scale in its rock cut sculptured architecture, Jainism has created a new style, and carried it to a pitch of excellence which places the glories of Mount Abu side by side with the mausoleum of the Taj among the architectural wonders of the world."

3. *On the 26th of February 1940 A.D. :* After an interval of fifteen years the grand festival of 'Mahāmastakābhisheka' was celebrated on the 26th of February 1940 A.D.

The significance of this grand ceremony was that it was wholly and solely managed for the first time by the Muzrai Department of the Mysore State, instead of the All-India Digambara Jaina Tirthakshetra Committee, Bombay, which had managed the preceding two 'Mahāmastakābhishekas', held in 1910 and 1925 A.D. The change-over in the management and control of the grand ceremony introduced this time has been continued to the present day. Of course, the State Government has established the practice of organizing the ceremony in close collaboration and co-operation with His Holiness Chārukirti Bhaṭṭāraka of Jaina Maṭha at Śravaṇa-Beḷagoḷa, the All India Digambara Jaina Tirthakshetra Committee, Bombay and other leading Associations of Jainas from different parts of the country.

The Government of Mysore by its order No. 877-28-2, dated 4th November 1938 A.D. sanctioned the holding of the 'Mahāmastakābhisheka' festival in February 1940 A.D. Accordingly the great festival began on 11th February 1940 A.D. with different preliminary ceremonies and reached its highest point on 26th February 1940 A.D., when the grand 'Mahāmastakābhisheka' ceremony was celebrated in the presence of about 2 lakhs of people who had specially assembled from all parts of the nation. The grand ceremony started at 9.30 a.m. on 26th February 1940 A.D., when the first 'Abhisheka', i.e., anointment of the image of Gommaṭeśvara was performed by His Highness Shri Krishṇa-Rājendra-Woḍeyār, the Mahārajā of Mysore, accompanied by the Prince Shri Jayachāmarājendra Woḍeyār. This time also His Highness Shri Krishṇa-Rājendra Woḍeyār opened the special session of the All India Digambara Jaina Mahasabha held on 26th February 1940.

The outstanding feature of the grand festival was that the 1008 'Kalaśas', used for the 'Mahāmastkābhisheka' ceremony were divided into four categories as follows :

1. Gold Kalaśas :	51
2. Silver Kalaśas :	300
3. German Silver Kalaśas :	300
4. Brass Kalaśas :	357
Total :	1008

All the Kalaśas were disposed of in auction. The first Gold Kalaśa of great honour was taken for Rs. 8001/- by Shri Kevalchand Ugrachand Doshi of Phaltan from Mahārāshtra. By the auction sale of these 'Kalaśas' over Rs. 75,000/- were collected and deposited with the Mysore Government. This amount is to be used for the protection and upkeep of the sacred image of Gommaṭeśvara.

4. *On the 5th of March 1953 A.D. :* The Government of Mysore by its Order No. S.R. 653-56-Muz. 188-48-6, dated the 2nd of May 1952 gave their sanction to hold the 'Mahāmastakābhisheka' ceremony in March 1953. Accordingly, two committees, viz., the 'Religious Committee' and the 'General Commit-

tee' were formed to organize and to conduct the celebrations. The Religious Committee under the chairmanship of His Holiness Chārukirtī Bhaṭṭāraka of Jaina Maṭha at Śravaṇa-Beḷagoḷa, was composed of prominent Jaina devotees like Sahu Shanti Prasad Jain of Calcutta and others. The Religious Committee was meant for looking after the religious affairs of the celebrations. The General Committee was formed with the Deputy Commissioner, Hassan District, as its Chairman and its main duties were to exercise control over the finances and to make all arrangements for providing facilities to the pilgrims.

This time the 1008 'Kalaśas', used for the 'Mahāmastakābhisheka' ceremony were divided into only 2 categories. viz., 900 silver Kalaśas and 108 Gold Kalaśas. The 900 Silver Kalaśas ware disposed of at a flat rate of Rs. 101/- each and the 108 Gold Kalaśas were disposed of in public auction. Further, four 'Chatushkoṇa Kuṁbhas' and 'Pushpavṛushṭi', i.e.. showering of flowers, were added as new items and were also disposed of by public auction. The first Gold Kalaśa of great honour was taken for Rs. 18,001 (as against Rs. 8,001/- on the previous occasion) by Shri Javanmal Sujanchand of Mensal from Bikaner in Rajasthan. The rest of the 107 Gold Kalaśas inclusive of four 'Chatushkoṇa Kumbhas' and 'Pushpavṛushṭi' were sold for different sums ranging from Rs. 121/- upto Rs. 5,501/-.

It is interesting to note that at the 1925 Mahāmastakābhisheka celebrations, out of 1008 Kalaśas only 546 Kalaśas were disposed of with a total realisation of Rs. 77,193/- whereas, for the 1953 celebrations the full number of Kalaśas were disposed of. In this way the total relaisations were Rs. 1,59,799/- as against the anticipated income of Rs. 1,00,000/-.

The preliminaries of the 'Mahāmastakābhishka' Ceremony commenced on the 18th of February 1953 and the great 'Abhisheka' was conducted in the ceremonious manner on the 5th of March 1953 in the presence of His Highness Shri Jaya-Chāmarājendra Woḍeyār, the Mahārājā of Mysore. In accordance with the time-honoured practice and the ardent wishes of the devotees the first pūjā to the sacred Image was performed by His Highness Shri Jaya-Chāmarājendra-Woḍeyār. After this first 'pūjā' Shri Javānmal Sujanchand of Mensal, Bikaner, conducted the 'pūjā' as he had offered the highest bid. The remaining devotees who had purchased the Kalaśas performed 'pūjās' in their turn.

The great rush of pilgrims from all parts of India commenced on the 25th of February 1953 and continued to increase from day to day. It reached the climax on the 4th and 5th of March 1953. On the 5th of March 1953 at about noon, the gathering was estimated at about 3 lakhs.

The remarkable feature of this festival was that many Jaina Associations held their special sessions or conferences during the period of the festival at Śravaṇa-Beḷagoḷa. The All-India Digambara Jaina Mahāsabhā held its special session on the occasion as they did on previous occasions. Similarly, the Jaina Young Mens' Association of Madras, the Jaina Mahilā Parishad of Bombay and the Vīra Sevā Mandir of Delhi held their special sessions by taking the opportunity of this great festival. But the most significant meetings were (i) the second session of the 'World Jaina Mission' held on the 5th of March 1950 which was attended by Hon'ble Shri Ajit Prasad Jain, the then Minister for Food Supplies and Rehabilitation, Government of India and the Hon'ble Minister for Education, Mysore State, and (ii) the second 'Cultural Conference of Ahiṁsā' held on the 6th of March 1953 which was addressed by the renowned Jaina scholar Principal A. Chakravartī of Madras. These two meetings were organised by the 'World Jaina Mission' under the inspiration of its Honorary Director, Shri Kamta Prasad Jain.

5. *On the 30th of March 1967 A.D.* : As per the practice started from the 1940 'Mahāmastakābhisheka' celebrations, the Muzrai Department of the Government of Mysore, organised the 'Mahāmastakābhisheka' ceremony on the 30th of March 1967. Accordingly, the 'Religious Committee' and the 'General Committee' were constituted to plan and to carry out the celebrations. In religious matters of the celebrations, the conspicuous thing, this time, was the encouraging presence of a large number of Jaina Sādhūs and Sādhvīs under the leadership of Āchāryaratna Deśabhūshaṇa Muni Mahārāj, the head of the Digambara Jaina ascetic order.

In keeping with the established practice, the 1008 Gold and Silver Kalaśas meant for the 'Mahāmastakābhisheka' ceremony were made available to the devotees through public auction and sale. The first Gold Kalaśa of great honour was taken in public auction for Rs. 47,500 (as against Rs. 18,001/- and Rs. 8,001/- on the preceding two occasions in 1953 and 1940, by Shri N.K. Jinachandran of Kalapattā in Kerala.

The preliminaries of the 'Mahāmastakābhisheka' ceremony commenced by 15th March 1967 and the great 'Mastakābhisheka' was conducted in the ceremonious manner on 30th March 1967 in the presence of Shri S. Nijalingappā, the then Chief Minister of Mysore, Dr. K.L. Shrimali, the then Vice-Chancellor of Mysore University, the Jaina ascetics and the heads of the Jaina Maṭhas. Shri N.K. Jinachandran performed the first 'pūjā' and poured the first Kalaśa of the 'Abhisheka' as he had offered the highest bid. The remaining devotees who had purchased the Kalaśas performed 'Abhisheka' in their turn. The entire ceremonies on this day were witnessed by a huge gathering which was estimated at about 5 lakhs.

The most spectacular and memorable feature of the celebrations on the 30th of March 1967 was 'Ākāśa Pushpavṛushṭī', i.e., the showering of flowers on the Image of Bāhubalī from the sky. This time for the purpose of showering flowers on the Image from the sky a novel and picturesque arrangement was made by specially procuring a helicopter from the Indian Air Force. This helicopter appeared on the scene at 10.30 A.M., came near the Image, remained stationary at about 20 feet above the 57 feet high Image of Bāhubalī and showered multicoloured flowers on the Image. Then the helicopter performed three 'Pradakshiṇās', i.e., it moved three times in a circle round the Image as a mark of profound devotion, again remained stationary above the Image in a specific position and once more showered the multicoloured flowers along with huge quantities of red vermilion and saffron colour powder in succession. As these coloured flowers and powders accurately fell on the colossal Image from the air, the entire gathering of about 5 lakhs was extremely thrilled with utmost joy and mental satisfaction and spontaneously gave expression to its feelings of reverence by loud shouts of 'Shri Bāhubalī Bhagawān ki Jai', i.e., 'victory to Lord Bāhubalī'. This 'Ākāśa Pushpavṛushṭī' was the most distinctive and unique event in the 1000 years' history of 'Mahāmastakābhisheka' celebrations. It was indeed a sight for the gods to see and the angels to admire.

For the first time the Government of India took a film of the entire 'Mahāmastakābhisheka' celebrations and this Indian News Reel film No. G. 65 was shown all over India from 7th to 13th April 1967. Similarly, some American and other foreign companies televised the different aspects of the 'Mahāmastakābhisheka' celebrations in their countries.

In accordance with the established practice, the 'All India Digambara Jaina Mahāsabhā' held its 72nd session on 31st March and 1st April 1967. In his inaugural speech, Dr. K.L. Shrimali, the former Minister for Education, Government of India and the then Vice-Chancellor of Mysore University, made a fervent plea for the scientific study of different aspects of Jainology and for establishing "Jaina Chairs" in different Universities for this purpose. It was also resolved in the session to organise a seminar of the heads of prominent Jaina educational institutions in India so as to evolve a uniform educational policy and programme among the Jainas. On the same lines, special sessions of 'Siddhānta Saṁrakshiṇī Sabhā', 'All India Mahilā Parishad", and 'All India Digambara Jain Tīrthkshetra Committee, Bombay' were also held.

6. *On the 22nd of February 1981 A.D.*: The programme of the 'Mahāmastakābhisheka' festival has been held in February-March 1981. The festival began from 9th February 1981 and continued upto the 20th of March 1981. The great 'Abhisheka' ceremony has taken place on 22nd February 1981. An extraordinary special signi ficance of historical nature has been attached to this ceremony as it marks the 1000th anniversary of the consecration of the Image of Bāhubalī, which was performed on Sunday 13th March 981 A.D. under the leadership of Military General and Chief Minister Chāmuṇḍa-Rāya who had installed this colossal image on the top of the Vindhyagiri hill at Śravaṇa-Beḷagoḷa. Obviously the preparations for the festival were made on an unprecedented grand scale in every respect. For this purpose a high power Committee termed as "Bhagwan Bāhubali Pratishṭhāpanā Sahasrābdi and Mahāmastakābhisheka Committee" was constituted under the Chairmanship of the most senior and respected Jaina leader Sahu Shriyans Prasad Jain of Bombay who is also the founder-President of All-India Digambara Jaina Mahāsamiti, Delhi. Further,

for looking after the religious a ffairs of the festival the Government of Karnāṭaka, as per established practice, had appointed a 'Religious Committee' with His Holiness Chārukīrti Bhaṭṭāraka Swāmī of Jaina Maṭha, Śravaṇa-Beḷagoḷa as its Chairman and Seth Lalchand Hirachand of Bombay (who is the President of 'All-India Digambara Jaina Tīrtha Kshetra Committee, Bombay) as its Vice-Chairman. The Government of Karnāṭaka, who have been managing such festivals from 1940 onwards, have been taking particular interest in this historic festival and as such have sanctioned five crores of rupees for arranging these celebrations and have out several improvements of permanent nature at Śravaṇa-Beḷagoḷa. The 'General Committee' appointed by the Government of Karnāṭaka had been looking after all these works of permanent constructions and development.

The entire work of planning and directing the schemes of '1000th Image Consecration Anniversary Celebrations' and of 'Mahāmastakābhisheka Ceremony' was carried out under the superb guidance and personal supervision of the world-renowned Jaina saint Elāchārya Munishree Vidyānand Mahārāj, who had been specially invited for these memorable celebrations by the Chief Minister of Karnāṭaka in view of the fact that the Munishree was the main architect behind the successful completion of the 'Bhagwān Mahāvira 2500th Nirvāṇ Mahotsava' was celebrations organised throughout the world during the year 1974-75 A.D. As a result, this historic festival of world-importance was arranged on a huge scale and for the first time the Prime Minister of India, Smt. Indira Gandhi, along with other Central Ministers and Chief Ministers of States, attended the celebrations on 21st Feb. 1981 and showered flowers from the helicopter on Bhagwan Bāhubalī. It was really a very happy coincidence of history that just as Siddhānta-Chakravartī Āchārya Nemichandra, who gave inspiration to his favourite disciple Chāmuṇḍa-Rāya to install the colossal image of Bāhubalī, guided the 'Pratishṭhhāpanā Mahotsava', i.e., the consecration ceremony, of the Image of Bāhubalī held on the 13th of March, 981 A.D., similarly Siddhānta-Chakravartī Elāchārya Munishree Vidyānand Mahārāj, who has been effectively spreading to the entire world the message of non-violence, self-control, renunciation and universal peace preached by Bāhubali, i.e., has guided the 'Pratishṭhāpanā Sahasrābdī Mahotsava', the Consecration's 1000th Anniversary Ceremony, of the Image of Bāhubali held on the 22nd of February, 1981 A.D.

In accordance with the time honoured traditional, practice, the 1008 'Kalaśas' meant for the 'Mahāmastakābhisheka' ceremony were made available to the devotees through sale at fixed prices. The 1008 Kalaśas had been divided into eight different categories and had been priced at different rates as follows :

Serial No.	*Type of Kalaśa*	*Number of Kalaśas*	*Amount to be paid for each Kalaśa Rs.*
1	Śatābdi Kalaśa	10	1,00,000/-
2	Divya Kalaśā	4	50,000/-
3	Ratna Kalaśa	4	25,000/-
4	Suvarṇa Kalaśa	200	11,000/-
5	Rajat Kalaśa	200	5,000/-
6	Tāmra Kalaśa	140	2,500/-
7	Kāsya Kalaśa	200	1,000/-
8	Gullikāy Ajgi Kalaśa	250	500/-
		1,008	

All the categories of Kalaśas had been purchased by the devotees. In this way the sale of Kalaśas created a record in the history of 'Mahāmastakābhisheka' festivals arranged during the last 1000 years.

Further, under the enlightened and broad lroad leadership of Elāchārya Munishree Vidyānand Mahārāj, the most novel and impressive scheme of "Jana-maṅgala Mahā-Kalaśa Pravartana" was launched. In a way, it marked the beginning of the 'Bāhubalı Pratishṭhāpanā Sahasrabdi Mahotsava', i.e., the 1000th Anniversary Celebrations of the Consecration of the Image of Bāhubalı, held on the 22nd of February, 1981, at Śravaṇa-Beḷagoḷa According to this scheme, an eight feet high holy copper urn was placed on a decorated chariot which started its travel from Delhi and passing through 110 major cities and towns of the country reached the destination of Śravaṇa-Beḷagoḷa on the 20th of February, 1981.

This 'Jana-maṅgala Mahā-kalaśa' was given a ceremonial send-off by Smt. Indira Gandhi, the Prime Minister of India on the 29th of September, 1980, at Red Fort grounds in Delhi. This 'Holy Urn' was accompanied by large groups of Jaina pilgrims, who, on the way, went on spreading the message of humanity, love and peace of Lord Bāhubalī,. who was the symbol of Indian culture which believed in tolerance, non-violence and national integration.

CHAPTER IX

GLORY OF ŚRAVAṆA BEḶAGOḶA

1. MATERIAL PROSPERITY

Śravaṇa-Beḷagoḷa occupied a very prominent position in the cultural history of India in general and of South India in particular. Śravaṇa-Beḷagoḷa has been considered by the Jainas all over India as one of their most sacred spots in this country. But the significance of Śravaṇa-Beḷagoḷa was not confined only to its popularity as a sacred place of Jaina pilgrimage It is clear that along with religious importance Śravaṇa-Beḷagoḷa had secular importance also as it was noted for its material, wealth and prosperity. In fact, Śravaṇa-Beḷagoḷa was widely known for its material affluence right from ancient times and its far-flung reputation as a centre of material abundance has been specifically stated in Inscription No. 1, engraved on the rock to the south of Pārśvanātha Basti on the Chikkapeṭṭa or Chandragiri hill at Śravaṇa-Beḷagoḷa dated about 600 A.D. in the following terms :

"Now indeed, after the sun Mahāvira who had risen to elevate the whole world had completely set, Bhadrabāhu Svāmī—of a lineage rendered illustrious by a succession of great men who came in regular descent from the venerable supreme 'rishī' Gautama-Gaṇadhara...and other teachers—who was acquainted with the true nature of the eight-fold great omens and was a seer of the past, the present and the future, having learnt from omen and foretold in Ujjayanī a calamity lasting for a period of twelve years, the entire 'saṅgha' (or community) set out from the North to the South and reached by degrees a country counting many hundreds of villages and filled with happy people, wealth, gold, grain, and herds of cows, buffaloes, goats and sheep".

In other words, when the celebrated Śrutakevalī Bhadrabāhu selected this southern centre of Śravaṇa-Beḷagoḷa for his 'Saṅgha' (or community), he made it clear to the world that the Jainas were going to a region that was economically self-sufficient and prosperous. Śravaṇa-Beḷagoḷa had continuously maintained this economic importance till recent times and then lost it, as many hundreds of centres have lost, because of the changed nature of the times and the onrush of the forces of the modern industrial world.

From close scrutiny of the epigraphs ranging from the twelfth to the sixteenth centuries A. D. it is evident that the commercial life of the people of Śravaṇa-Beḷagoḷa was marked by some special features. The most noticeable of those was their intense devoutness and patriotism. It is a fact that in early and medieval times in the South, patriotism went hand in hand with religion. The merchants of Śravaṇa-Beḷagoḷa were no exception to this rule. For example, according to Inscriptions Nos. 241 and 242, dated about 1175 A.D., all the merchants of Śravaṇa-Beḷagoḷa had pledged themselves to pay annually for as long as the sun, moon and stars endure, certain specified contributions, to provide for flowers for Gommaṭa-deva and Pārśvadeva. These merchants, it is stated, were "endowed with all good qualities", and are said in the two inscriptions to have been "of the holy place Beḷuguḷa." It is interesting to observe in this connection that it was not only men who thus gave evidence of their devoutness, but women as well. One of these two epigraphs expressly relates as follows : "To provide for flowers for Gommaṭadeva, all the merchants of the holy place Baḷuguḷa, including Gumi-Setti's Dāsaiyā, Lokeya-Sahāṇī's daughter Somavve and others, having purchased certain lands at Gaṅgasamudra and Gommaṭapura from the assembly, made over the same to the garland-maker with a charter to the effect that he was to enjoy them for as long as the sun, moon and stars endure." In the like manner, the merchants of Mosale, probably a neighbouring place, also shared their devotion. For in the Inscription No. 236, dated about 1185 A.D., it is clearly mentioned that the merchants of Mosale pledged themselves to give annually, as a perpetual gift, certain specified amounts for the eight kinds of worship of the Tīrthaṅkaras, set up by Basavi Seṭṭi. the large-hearted Jaina merchant leader of Śravaṇa-Beḷagoḷa.

Further, it is interesting to note that, in the Inscription No. 235, dated about 1185 A.D., the above-named merchant Basavi-Seṭṭi has been called *'Vaḍḍa-Vyavahārī'*, i.e., the senior-most merchant, which obviously suggests that the merchants of Mosale had gradations of honour amonst them. This system of gradation is also clear from the Inscription No. 397, which is assigned to about 1179 A.D., stating that the merchant by name Malli-Seṭṭi was the *'Paṭṭaṇasvāmī'*, i.e., the Lord Mayor, of Gommaṭapura. Thus from these records it is evident that the Jainas of Śravaṇa-Beḷagoḷa were organized in commercial guilds and that the merchants of the holy place led a corporate life.

Ths merchants of this holy place were also famous for certain virtues. This fact has been specifically mentioned in the Incription No. 335, dated 1195 A.D., as follows : "The merchants were born in the eminent line of Khandali and Mulabhondra, devoted to truth and purity, possessed of lion's valour, skilled in conducting various kinds of trade with many seaports, adorned with the famous three jewels, the marchants residing at the holy place Beḷuguḷa acquired celebrity on earth."

From the same lengthy Inscription No. 335, dated 1195 A.D. we learn about another special feature of the commerciial life of the merchants of Śravaṇa-Beḷagoḷa. This is related to the very high place they occupied in the civic life of the people. The merchants of Śravaṇa-Beḷagoḷa were in charge of the religious endowments of that city. The same record informs us that the merchants of that centre "were the protectors of the Jinālaya", i.e., the famous Nagara-Jinālaya of Śravaṇa-Beḷagoḷa.

Even in later years the merchants of Śravaṇa-Beḷagoḷa were in charge of the public charities of that centre. Thus in Inscription No. 244, dated about 1274 A.D., it is specifically mentioned that as per agreement the jewel merchants of Śravaṇa-Beḷagoḷa were to look after the charity which was made by some one whose name is not mentioned in the epigraph. But we are informed that a perpetual endowment of four *'gadyānas'* was made as an act of reverence to the memory of Medhāvī Seṭṭi of

Barakanur, the lay disciple of Prabhāchandra Bhaṭṭāraka, with the condition that three maṇas' of milk should be supplied every day as long as the sun and the moon lasted. Similarly, this kind of arrangement with the special responsibility of the jewel merchants of Śravaṇa-Beḷagoḷa has been categorically stated in the Inscription No. 245, dated about 1274 A.D., as follows" : "Keṭī-Seṭṭi son of Soy-Seṭṭi of Halasur, paid 3 '*gadyānas*' to provide for 3 'maṇas' of milk for the daily anointment of Gommaṭadeva. The milk should be supplied out of the interest on the sum by the jewel merchants for as long as the sun and moon last. Good fortune."

The extreme care with which the merchants looked after the public charities entrusted to their charge is proved by the agreement mentioned in the Inscription No. 336, dated 1288 A.D., which states: "All the jewel merchants of the holy place of Beḷuguḷa and Jinanāthapura, agreeing upon themselves, gave a deed as follows: "For the repairs (of the temple) of the god Ādi of the Nagara Jinālaya. temple vessels, etc. and services all the merchants of those two cities granted, with pouring of water, to continue for as long as the sun, the moon, and the stars endure, '*davana*' at the rate of one *gadyāna*' for every hundred '*gadyāns*' of '*davana*' received from either local men or foreigners, for the god Ādi." The concluding lines of this deed clearly prove the solidarity of the merchants, their intense patriotism, and their honesty of purpose. They state : "If any one denies or conceals (his income) in this matter, his race shall be childless, he shall be a traitor to the god, a traitor to the king, and a traitor to the creed. The signature of all the merchants. —Śrī Gommaṭa."

The existence of jewel merchants and their guild for centuries at Śravaṇa-Beḷagoḷa bespeaks great wealth and influence in that centre. But wealth brought with it pleasure and enjoyment, and in this connection one more feature of Śravaṇa-Beḷagoḷa can be mentioned. It is with reference to the existence of dancing girls in that city. These were in no way behind other citizens in their piety and large-heartedness. An example of one such generous and devout dancing girl was that of Maṅgāyi. The two Inscriptions Nos. 339 and 341, dated about 1325 A.D., relate that she was the disciple of Abhinava-Chārukīrtī-Paṇḍitāchārya and that she was "a crest-jiwel of firm faith (in Jainism), and a crest-jewel of royal dancing girls." This devout dancing girl Maṅgāyī caused a famous *Chaityālaya,* i.e., temple-named Tribhuvanachūḍāmaṇī to be built at Śravaṇa-Beḷagoḷa. For nearly two centuries this wonderful structure received public donations and charities.

2. SPIRITUAL UNIVERSITY

Śravaṇa-Beḷagoḷa was distinguished more as a spiritual centre than for its material abundance right from the time of Bhadrabāhu in the third century B.C. Since the place was hallowed both by the sacred presence and by the ultimate death in accordance with the supreme rite of 'Sallekhanā' of Śruta-kevalī Bhadrabāhu, the highest religious and spiritual authority of the time, and his disciple, Emperor Chandragupta Maurya, as a Jaina ascetic by name Chandragupta Muni, it became the first most important '*tīrtha-kshetra*', i.e., the holy place and the place of pilgrimage, in South India as early as the third century B.C. Again, due to its calm, peaceful and picturesque natural surroundings the place was ideally suited for leading an ascetic life of contemplation and meditation and for carrying out educational activities of learning, teaching and writing. As a result Śravaṇa-Beḷagoḷa soon became a prominent centre of religious and educational activities under the able guidance of renowned saints and talented preceptors and it assumed the status of a virtual spiritual university. This supreme position in the important religious and educational activities was successfully maintained by Śravaṇa-Beḷagoḷa continuously for centuries during the ancient and medieval period, as it was closely associated with the very eminent and hightly learned Jaina ascetics, popularly known as '*gurus*'.

Fortunately, the succession lists of such Jaina 'gurus' have been mentioned in about a dozen inscriptions at Śravaṇa-Beḷagoḷa. These inscriptions give, in addition to the names of 'gurus' some interesting items of information about the learning, authorship and polemical skill of the 'gurus' the kings or chiefs by whom they were honoured, the manner in which they ended their life, and so forth. The earliest inscription (i.e. No.62) containing a list of 'gurus' is dated about 900 A.D., and the last inscription of this type (i.e. No. 258) is dated 1432 A.D. It means that, for a period of five centuries, the practice of giving succession lists of Jaina 'gurus' was maintained. Obviously such lists are not only very informative but also immensely useful from the historical point of view, as they contain authentic records of the time. For example, in the Inscription No. 64, dated 1163 A.D., the spiritual descent of 'Gurus' is given as follows :

Gautam and others
(In their line)
Bhadrabāhu
|
Chandragupta
(In this line)
Kondakunda alias Padmanandī
(In his line)
Umāsvāti alias Gṛidhrapichchha
|
Balākapichchha
(In his line)
Samantabhadra
(Then)
Pūjyapāda alias Devanandī alias Jinendrabuddhi
(Then)
Akalaṅka
(In his line)
Gollāchārya
|
Traikālyayogi
Kumāradeva alias Aviddhakarna-Padmanandī
|
Kulabhūshaṇa | Prabhāchandra
|
Kulachandra
|
Māghanandī
|
Gandavimuktadeva
|
Devakīrtī (died in 1163 A.D.)
|
Tribhuvanadeva,

Further, such inscriptions giving succession lists of Jaina 'gurus' also provide greatly valuable information in brief about their scholastic and other achievements. The specific information of this type about some of important gurus as mentioned in these inscriptions is as follows :

1. *Kundakunda* : He was the leader of the 'Mūla-saṅgha' congregation of the ascetics. Inscription No. 127, dated 1115 A.D., states that he had the power of walking in the sky. This is mentioned in several other records also. Again, Inscription No. 351, dated 1119 A D., states that he walked in the sky four inches above the earth and Inscription No. 254, dated 1398 A.D., gives a poetical explanation of this by saying that he did so in order to show that he was not touched in the least both within and without by dust (or passion), the earth being the abode of dust.

2. *Umāsvāti :* He is the author of *Tattvārthasūtra* and is also known as 'Griddhapichchāchārya'.

3. *Samantabhadra :* He is termed as 'Vādī-simha' (i.e. a lion in disputation) and as 'Samasta-vidyānidhi' (i.e., a repository of all learning). It is stated that he destroyed the disease known as 'bhasmaka', and his eagerness for, and skill in, disputations are thus described in his own words : "At first the drum was beaten by me (as a challenge to disputants) in the city of Pāṭaliputra, and afterwards in the country of Mālava, Sindhu and Ṭhakka (i.e. the Punjab), at Kāñchī and at Vidishā (i.e. Bhilsa). I have now arrived a tKarahāṭaka (i.e. Karaḷāda= Karāda) Desirous of disputation, O King, I exhibit the sporting of a tiger. When the disputant Samantabhadra stands in thy court, O King, even the tongue of Dhūrjaṭi (i.e. Śiva) who talks clearly and skilfully, turns back quickly towards the nape of the neck. What hope can there be for others ?"

4. *Śivakoṭī :* He was a disciple of Samantabhadra and the author of a commentary on *Tattvārthasūtra.*

5. *Akalaṅka :* He defeated the Buddhists in disputation and overcame '*Tārā*' who had become secretly manifest in a pot.

6. *Vakragrīva :* He expounded the meaning of the word '*atha*' (i.e. then) for six months.

7. *Simhanandī :* He was the founder of the Gaṅga kingdom,

8. *Māghanandī :* He was the founder of the 'tīrtha'

at Kolhāpur.

9. *Pūjyapāda :* He was so called because his feet were worshipped by the forest deities. At first named Devanandī by his 'guru' he was subsequently known as 'Jinendra buddhi' since he was endowed with universal intelligence like Jina. He was the author of the 'Jainendra Grammar', the 'Sarvārtha-siddhi', which is a commentary on 'Tattvārthasūtra', the 'Jinābhisheka', and the 'Samādhiśataka'. It is stated of Pūjyāpāda that he was unrivalled in the power of healing and that the water in which his feet were washed could transform iron into gold.

10. *Gopanandī :* He is said to have been a great poet and a logician; he caused the Jaina religion, which had for a long time been at a stand-still, to attain the prosperity and fame of the time of the Gaṅga kings—an achievement which was quite impossible for any one else.

11. *Prabhāchandra :* He was honoured by King Bhoja of Dhārā. He was the author of a celebrated work on logic. It is also stated that Śāntalā Devi, the chief queen of Hoyasala monarch Vishṇuvardhana, was the lay disciple of Prabhā-chandra.

12. *Dāmanandi :* He is described as the vanquisher of the great disputant Vishṇubhaṭṭa.

13. *Jinachandra :* He was as though a Pūjyapāda in the Jainendra grammar, a Bhaṭṭākalaṅka in logic and a Bhāravi in literature.

14. *Trimushṭideva :* He was so called because he was content with three fistfuls of food.

15. *Vāsavachandra :* It is stated that he attained celebrity as 'Bāla-Saraswatī' in the Chālukya capital.

16. *Yashahkīrtī :* He was honoured by the king of Siṁhala, i.e., Ceylon or Shri Lanka.

17. *Gollāchārya :* Before becoming an ascetic Gollāchārya was the ruler of the Golla country and belonged to the family of King Mutana-Chaṇḍila.

18. *Traikālyayogī :* He is said to have made a Brahma-rākshasa his pupil and converted the oil of 'honge' tree (pongamia glabra) into pure ghee. The very thought of him drove away evil spirits.

19. *Meghachandra-traividya :* He is described as an equal of Jinasena and Vīrasena in philosophy, as Akalaṅkadeva himself in the six schools of logic, and as Pūjyapāda himself in grammar.

20. *Śruta-kīrti :* He astonished the learned by composing the 'Rāghava-Pāṇḍavīyam' in such a way that it could be read both forwards and backwards.

21. *Śruta-muni :* He is described as a Pūjyapāda in grammar, as an Akalaṅka in logic and as a Kunda-kunda in the knowledge of the self.

22. *Ajita-sena :* He bore the title 'Vādibha-Siṁha' and was the preceptor of the great commander-in-chief Chāmuṇḍa-Rāya and of his son, Jinadevana. It is said that he directed Chāmuṇḍa-Rāya to give the name of Beḷagoḷa to the village where the image of Bāhubalī was erected. He was also known as Ajitasena-Bhaṭṭāraka.

These great Jaina saints were associated, in one way or the other, with the sacred place of Śravaṇa-Beḷagoḷa. Obviously, this kind of continued association raised the importance of this holy place to that of a spiritual centre. In addition, the Jaina saints who resided at Śravaṇa-Beḷagoḷa paid considerable attention to scholarship and learning. In the difficult subjects like Grammar, Poetry, Prosody, Siddhānta, Medicine and Logic, these saints of Śravaṇa-Beḷagoḷa strove to achieve distinction, and they devoted their quiet lives in the pursuit of learning. The best representative of such celebrated saints is Siddhānta-Chakravartī Nemichandra. He composed at Śravaṇa-Beḷagoḷa his reputed philosophical treatises entitled (1) *Dravya-saṅgraha* (2) *Gommaṭasāra-Jīva-kāṇḍa.* (3) *Gommaṭasāra-Kārma-Kāṇḍa,* (4) *Labdhisāra,* (5) *Kshapaṇāsāra and* (6) *Trilokasāra.* He also wrote a work named *Pratishṭhāpāṭha,* which consists directions for the establishment and consecration of images. In his works he always makes obeisance to his preceptors, viz., Abhaya-nandī, Indra-nandī, Vīra-nandī, and Kanaka-nandī. Due to these classic and standared philosophical treatises, Nemichandra was popularly known as 'Siddhānta-Chakravartī', i.e., 'the Paramount Lord of the Philosophy'. But Nemichandra is still better known as the preceptor of Chāmuṇḍa-Rāya, the chief minister and millitary General of the Gaṅga kingdom. In fact Chāmuṇḍa-Rāya was his most favourite disciple, and we find that Nemichandra composed his one philosophical treatise according to the desire of Chāmuṇḍa-Rāya, who wished to learn the exposition of substances as enumerated in the canonical works of the Jainas and that he named it 'Gommaṭasāra' as it was composed for the reading of Chāmuṇḍa-Rāya, who was also known as Gommaṭa-Rāya. This intimate relationship between Nemichandra and Chāmuṇḍa-Rāya is best expressed in a verse in an inscription dated about 1530 A.D., engraved in the enclosure of Padmāvatī temple in Nagar Talukā of Shimogā District as follows :

मिलोकसार-प्रमुख:.........

भुवि नेमिचन्द्र: ।

विभाति सैद्धान्तिक-सार्वभोम:

चामुण्डराजाधित-पादपद्म: ।

i.e. "(The author of) Trilokasāra and other works...... Nemichandra the Saiddhāntika Sārvabhauma (the Paramount Lord of those versed in the Siddhāntas) shines in this world, his lotus-feet worshipped by Chāmuṇḍa-Rāya". Though a fragment of this verse is effaced, the meaning is quite clear. The 'Saiddhāntika Sārvabhauma' is a synonym of the epithet ' Siddhānta-Chakravartī", generally applied to Nemichandra. Further, at the instance of Āchārya Nemichandra, Chāmuṇḍa-Rāya installed the colossal image of Bāhubali on the Vindhyagiri hill and performed its consecration ceremony on the 13th of March 981 A.D. under his personal guidance. Again, according to tradition, Chāmuṇḍa-Rāya, after erecting the colossal image, appointed his guru Nemichandra as the head of the *Maṭha* i.e., monastery, at Śravaṇa-Beḷagoḷa. Moreover, out of the two figures sculptured below the inscription on the pillar, known as Tyāgada Brahmadeva Pillar, on the Vindhyagiri hill, the one flanked by Chauri-bearers is said to represent Chāmuṇḍa-Rāya and the other his guru Nemichandra. Obviously, this close association of an eminent saint like Nemichandra with Śravaṇa-Beḷagoḷa greatly enhanced the prestige of the place as a spiritual and educational centre.

Apart form this intimate relationship between Śravaṇa-Beḷagoḷa and the most reputed saints for centuries, the place was known for its treasure of manuscripts. For example, the temple situated in the west of the enclosure of Akkana-basti in the village Śravaṇa-Beḷagoḷa was termed as 'Siddhānta-Basti', because practically all the books bearing on the Jaina 'Siddhānta', i.e., philosophy were once secured in a dark room of this 'Basti'. It is obvious that the learned Āchārya like Nemichandra must have taken advantage of this great treasure of knowledge. It is also likely that this treasure must have been useful to Nemichandra in his writing of high philosophical treatises like Gommaṭasāra. It is said that, at some remote period, Dhavalā, Jaya-dhavalā and other rare philosophical works were carried away from Śravaṇa-Beḷagoḷa to Mūḍabidrī in the South Kanara District. Any way, Śravaṇa-Beḷagoḷa did contribute to the sacred work of the preservation of rare manuscripts for a long period. Thus the availability of rare manuscripts for study also increased the position of Śravaṇa-Beḷagoḷa as a religious and educational centre.

In addition, the Jaina '*Maṭha*' at Śravaṇa-Beḷagoḷa rendered great services in the field of religious and educational activities. This 'Maṭha' along with similar Maṭhas at Mūḍabidrī, Kārkal, Hūmachā, Kolhāpur, Nāndaṇī, Malakheḍ and several other places in India, was established in the early medieval period and was revived by Chāmuṇḍa-Rāya after the installation of the colossal image of Bāhubali on the Vindhyagiri hill of the village. The head pontiff of this Maṭha is known by the traditional name of Svastiśrī Chārukīrti Bhaṭṭāraka, but he is popularly called 'Paṇḍitārya' or 'Paṇḍitāchārya' or 'Swāmigaḷu'. According to tradition this Bhaṭṭāraka used to perform a number of duties of a religious nature. In the field of religion he not only directed and controlled the religious behaviour of his followers, but also encouraged and helped the undertaking and completion of various religious projects and activities. He ably discharged his responsibility to provide religious education to students and others by various means like conducting *Pāṭha-śālās*, i.e., religious schools, maintaining *Śāstra-bhāṇḍras*, i.e., religious scripture libraries, delivering *Dharma-pravachanas*, i.e., religious discourses, publishing and distributing *Dharmagranthas*. i.e., religious books, training persons in the performance of *Dharma-vidhīs*, i.e., religious rituals, arranging *Dharma-sammelanas*, i.e., religious conferences, etc. Further, it was his main work to supervise and direct several relgious functions like *Mūrti-pratishṭhāpanā*, i.e., installation of images in temples, and various *Dharma-Samārambhas*, i.e., religious ceremonies. Similarly, he used to officiate at all kinds of *Pūjās*, i.e., worships, and especially at the great *Vrata-Udyāpana-Pūjās*, i.e., the special worships arranged at the completion of religious vows. On the same lines, the Bhaṭṭāraka always performed, personally or through others, important *Dharma-Saṁskāras*, i.e., religious sacraments, at the time of birth, marriage and death. Moreover, the major concern of the Bhaṭṭāraka was to look after the management of the *Tīrthakshetra*, i.e., the holy place of Śravaṇa-Beḷagoḷa. Furthermore, the Bhaṭṭāraka invariably devoted particular attention to encourage and help his followers in carrying out religious activities like construction of new temples, renovation of old temples, grant of donations, publication of books, provision of education, medicine and shelter to the needy, organization of facilities and conveniences to the pilgrims, maintenance of proper relations with the government. etc. As these multifarious duties of a religious nature were carried out on a large scale continuously for centuries by the religious authority like the Bhaṭṭāraka in the general interest of the followers of the religion, the significance of Śravaṇa-Beḷagoḷa as a strong-hold of religious activities was constantly maintained. In fact, the Jaina Maṭha at Śravaṇa-Beḷagoḷa had always been a very prominent centre of Jaina religion and culture. Naturally, this institution of the Bhaṭṭāraka also helped a great deal in maintaining and enhancing the reputation of Śravaṇa-Beḷagoḷa as a spiritual university.

Further, the extra-ordinary importance of Śravaṇa-Beḷagoḷa as a highly prominent spiritual centre is quite evident from the fact that all categories of persons like the rulers and the ruled, the rich and the poor, the learned and the illiterate, the 'Sādhūs and the Sādhvīs', i.e., the monks and the nuns, and the 'Śrāvakas and the Śrāvikās', i.e., the lay men and the lay women, considered it of immense value to lead a restrained life in accordance with the vows laid down in the scriptures and especially to voluntarily quit the life as per the religious rite of 'Sallekhanā' at the most sacred and hallowed place of Śravaṇa-Beḷagoḷa. *Sallekhana* is a specific way in which death is brought about strictly under certain specifc conditions, by the performance of a vow. *Sallekhanā* is described by Āchārya Samantabhadra in his authoritative work entitled *Ratnakaraṇḍa Śrāvakāchāra* as follows: "When overtaken by a calamity, by famine, by old age, or by an incurable disease, to get rid of the body for 'dharma' is called 'Sallekhanā. One should by degrees give up solid food and take liquid food; then, giving up liquid food one should gradually content oneself with warm water; then, abandoning even warm water, one should fast entirely, and thus, with mind intent on the 'pañchanamaskāra', i.e., five salutations, should by every effort quit the body".

There are ample evidences to show that many devout Jainas willingly submitted themselves to the inevitable death by the rite of *Sallekhanā* at Śravaṇa-Beḷagoḷa. There are about ninety epitaphs, that is inscriptions, which record the death of men and women, mostly monks and nuns, by the performance of 'Sallekhanā'. The epitaphs range in date from about 600 to 1809 A.D. Of these epitaphs about sixty-four commemorate the death of men, mostly monks, and sixteen mention the death of women, mostly nuns. In a few cases the period of the fast is mentioned: one month each in epitaphs Nos. 25, 143 and 167; twenty-one days in No. 33, and three-days in No. 59. About seventy-five per cent of these epitaphs belong to the seventh and eighth centuries A.D. Of these epitaphs many are important as they furnish some additional informoation. For example, Inscription No. 1 records the death of a Jaina guru named Prabhāchandra on the mountain named Kaṭavapra, i.e., Chandragiri hill and states that in course of time seven hundred 'ṛshis' or ascetics similarly accomplished *Samādhi*, i.e., voluntary death. Again, the Inscription No. 11 mentions the name of a king who was present at the time of his guru's death by 'Sallekhanā'. Among the monks whose death by 'Sallekhanā' is recorded in the early epitaphs may be mentioned: (1) Akshaya-kīrti of Southern Madhurā, who was bitten by a snake; (vide Inscription No. 27, dated about 700 A.D.); (2) Śāntisena-muni, who revived the Jaina faith when it had become weak after the time of sages Bhadrabāhu and Chandragupta; (vide Inscription No. 31, dated about 650 A.D.); and (3) Chandradevāchārya, renowned in the Nāḍi kingdom (vide Inscription No. 84, dated about 700 A.D.). Among the later epitaphs mention may be made af Inscription No. 127 which records the death in 1115 A.D. of a famous saint by name Meghachandra-traividyadeva of the Pustaka-gachchha, of the Deśīyagaṇa. of the Mūla-Saṅgha, and a disciple of Āchārya Sakalendu. After giving a succession of gurus from Gautama-gaṇadhara to Meghachandra who is praised at length, the record closes with the statement that Prabhāchandra, the chief disciple of Meghachandra, had the epitaph consecrated with great magnificance through his lay disciples Gaṅga-Rāja (the great General and chief Minister of Hoyasala Kingdom) and his wife Lakshmī-Devī. Again, Inscription No. 140 states that Prabhāchandra, the disciple of Meghachandra, died in 1145 A.D. Here his lay disciple Śāntalā-Devī, the chief queen of Vishṇuvardhana, is mentioned and reference is made to the death of her mother, Māchikabbe. Further, Inscription No. 254 gives information about the transmission of the sacred love and the formation of the 'saṅghas', (i.e., the congregations of ascetics), its object being to record the death in 1398 A.D. of a guru named Paṇḍita. Similarly, Inscription No. 258 refers to the formation of 'Saṅghas' and records the death in 1432 A.D. of Śruta-muni and unlike other epitaphs also mentions the death by the rite of 'Sallekhanā' of four of his predecessors. We also learn that 'Śruta-muni was suffering from an incurable disease, and his reflections on the evanescent nature of the world before death are given in detail.

Thus it is clear that, in order to end their life by the rite of 'Sallekhanā', persons used to come to Śravaṇa-Beḷagoḷa from the north and from various places in the south. Obviously, it reveals the utmost significance attached by the people to Śravaṇa-Beḷagoḷa as a spiritual centre.

Moreover, the records of the pilgrims also clearly reveal the tremendous spiritual importance that they attached to Śravaṇa-Beḷagoḷa. There are many inscriptions, numbering about 160, which record the visits of pilgrims from southern and northern India. These records may not be very important historically, but they have their own value in several other respects, one of them, for example, being their antiquity. They thus bear unequivocal testimony to the sacredness and importance of the place even in early times, so that eminent Jaina gurus, poets, artists, chiefs of the army, officers and other high personages in common with ordinary people deemed it a duty to visit the place, at least once in their life time, and to have their names permanently recorded on the holy spot.

CHAPTER-X

CONTRIBUTIONS OF ŚRAVAṆA-BEḶAGOḶA

1. SUBLIME AND MEANINGFUL SCULPTURE

Śravaṇa-Beḷagoḷa has been famous in the world for the last so many centuries for its lasting contributions to the culture of the world through its ideal saints, classic philosophical works, exquisite sacred monuments like temples, caves, pillars, etc., and especially the impressive colossal image of Gommaṭeśvara. Śravaṇa-Beḷagoḷa is the well-known temple-city of the Jainas in India as it contained innumerable shrines situated on the Vindhyagiri hill, on the Chandragiri hill, in the village proper and in the adjacent villages like Jinanāthapura and Kambaḍa-haḷḷi. These shrines, as per the established practice in South India, have been divided broadly into two categories, viz., '*Bastis*' and '*Beṭṭas*'. This division of the southern Jaina shrines into two classes, called Bastis and Beṭṭas, is the major peculiarity that distinguishes the Jaina architecture of South India from that of North India. The term 'Basti', properly 'Basadi', signifies a Jaina temple; and it is the Kannaḍa form of the Sanskrit word 'Vasati' having the same meaning. Hence 'Bastis' are temples, in the usual acceptance of the word in North India, containing images of one or more of the twenty-four Tīrthaṅkaras which are the usual objects of worship. On the other hand, the term 'Beṭṭa', in the Kannaḍa language, literally means a hill; but it is used in a specific sense by the Jainas in South India. Here the term 'Beṭṭa' is applied to a special form of shrine consisting of a courtyard open to the sky, with cloisters round about and in the centre a colossal image, not of a Tīrthaṅkara, but of a saint and usually of the saint Bāhubalī, the son of the first Tīrthaṅkara, Lord Ṛishabhadeva. Hence the colossal image of Bāhubali on the Vindhyagiri hill belongs to the category of 'Beṭṭas' and provides the best and most ancient example of such 'Beṭṭas'. This colossal and dignified image of Bāhubalī, which is one of the largest free-standing images in the world, is the most distinctive contribution of Śravaṇa-Boḷagoḷa to the culture of the world both from the sculptural point of view as the magnificent creation of art in the world and from the philosophical point of view through the message of eternal values it gives to the world.

The colossal image of Gommṭeśvara is the most impressive and wonderful image in the world because of its huge size of 57 feet in height and of its location on the crest of the Vindhyagiri hill which rises over 450 feet above the level of the ground. Due to its unique size and location, this image, unlike other images, is visible from a distance of about 10 miles all around. It is carved out of a tall granitic tor which was originally on the hill-top and which amply satisfied the sculptor by its homogeneity and fine grained texture. The sculpture is finished in the round from the head down to the region of the thighs by the removal of the unwanted rock from behind, front and sides. Below the thighs, the knees and the feet are cut in very high relief with the parent rock-mass still left on the flanks and rear, as if to support it. The flanking rockmasses depict ant-hills and 'Kukkuṭa-sarpas', i.e., cocktrices emerging out and from among them, and on either side emerges a 'mādhavī' creeper climbing up to entwine the legs and thighs and ascending almost to the arms, near the shoulders, with their leaves spaced out and terminating in a cluster of flowers or berries. The pedestal on which stand the feet of Gommaṭa, each measuring a feet, is a full-blown lotus, Broad-chested and majestic, Gommaṭa stands erect in the 'Khaḍgāsana'-pose with his arms dangling on either side reaching to the knees and with thumbs facing in. The carving of the almost rounded head, 7.6 feet high, erect, facing the north, with a sublime compoure, is a most marvellous composition of any age. The half-closed and contemplative eyes, with their gaze turned towards the tip of the sharp and sensitive nose, the well-shaped pouting lips wearing a benign and serene smile, the slightly-projected chin wlth a dimple above. an imperceptibly high cheek, lobed ears and subdued and voluted curls of locks on the head invading the broad forehead-all make for a charming face, yet quite serene. The broad shoulders, 26 feet across, of sturdy appearance and the lack of well-modulated elbow and knee joints, the broad and slightly heaved up chest, the narrow hip, about 10 feet wide in front, the wider pelvis, about 13 feet across in front, and rounded gluteal bulges, as if to balance the erect stance, the incurved and channelled midline of the back, the firmly-planted pair of feet, in brief all the *mahāpurushalakshaṇas* in the best proportion, accentuate the beauty of the modelling and the grace of the stance, while at the same time they indicate the conventions of Jaina iconography adopted in respect of the Tīrthaṅkaras' forms that had to eschew undue emphasis on corporeal graces tending to the worldly and voluptuous. The sculptor has very effectively brought into existence in stone the concept of *mahāpurusha* with all the *aṅga-lakshaṇas*. The nudity of the figure, indicating absolute renunciation of a 'Kevalin', i.e., omniscient, the stiff erectness of the stance, suggesting firm determination and self-control of a Jina, and the beaming smile and a contemplative gaze—all blend together to bring out the greatness of conception and the mastery of the sculptor. The deft skill with which the head and its mien, the crease lines on the neck and the palm lines, the hands, the fingers, even the nails and the feet with their toe and nails are delineated in this hard intractable 'in situ' rock is something to be marvelled at.

Further, as a masterpiece of monoliths the image of Gommṭeśvara is unrivalled in the world. The Egyptian colossi, including that of Ramses, as also the great Buddhas on the faces of the cliffs of Bamian in Afganistan, are at best reliefs, while the Gommaṭeśvara is in the round for most of its height above the knees, with a rear side as perfectly shaped and modelled as the front side. Further, this sculpture is cut and is wrought out of the hardest stone as compared to the above reliefs carved in much softer sand stone or lime stone.

Added to this is the mirror-like smooth aud shining polish of the entire body that brings out the rich fine grains of this greyish white granite, an art that had been lost or forgotten for more than a millennium since the workmen of Ashoka had polished the extensive interiors of the Ājīvika caves in the hills near Gayā in north India. For a hypaethral statue on a high hill-top exposed to sun, rain, heat, cold and abrasive dust and rain-carrying winds the polish acts as a great refractory—a fact which the makers seem to have understood. Unlike the earlier examples of Gommaṭa at Ellora and other places, the creepers entwining round the body have been shown here with great control with their distinctive foliage well-spaced apart and in a way that would not detract from the majesty of the main figure itself.

Thus this colossal image of Bāhubalī is known as a marvellous creation of art, unsurpassed so far in the whole world. But this image is still more significant in the world for the message of eternal values which it gives to the entire humanity. The image, though huge, is so expressive that apart from its total effect of awe and serenity, its different features also invariably convey certain profound meanings which create a deep impact on the visitors even within a very short period of their visit. For instance, the stiff erectness of the image in the 'Kāyotsarga' posture indicates perfect self-control and firm self-confidence, the faint and benign smile of the face indicates complete inward bliss and utmost sympathy for the suffering world, the nudity of the figure suggests absoulte renunciation and full detachment from the world, and the huge size of the figure reveals the greatness of the saint and at the same time it creates the feelings of hope in man that he also can achieve similar greatness by following the path of penance laid down by him. Its 'bhavya', i.e., grand pose its 'vītarāga'. i.e., impassive face, its equisite appearance and its meditative mood are really exemplary. Even though it is one thousand years old, it looks extremely beautiful and bright, as though quite fresh from the chisel of the artist. It creates such a deep impact of superb feelings on the mind which even the reading of scriptures would not be in a position to do. Naturally, this image evokes in the minds of the visitors utmost admiration for the unknown artist, who carved it, and for the commander-in chief Chāmuṇḍa-Rāya, who installed it.

Further, the very sight of the image gives a kind of profound spiritual bliss and mental satisfaction to us. If ever and anywhere stone can speak, it certainly speaks here for all times. Nay, it does more. It instils in us feelings of devotion, piety and humility. It makes us bold to shun all forms of hypocrisy and sin, and strengthens us to walk on the path of righteousness. Obviously, the sublime statue creates at once deep feelings of compelling reverence and complete submission. For example, there have been many instances when the fierce iconoclasts who rushed up the hill to mutilate the image, had, on seeing it, to throw their axes aside and stand ashamed in mute reverence. That is why during the long period of Muslim domination in South India, this image, unlike the images at Hampī, Koppal, Lakkuṇḍī and other sacred places in Karnāṭaka, remained throughout unhurt and unmutilated. Similarly, this image did evoke pious feelings in the minds of foreign dignitaries also. The great general Sir Arthur Wellesley who was commanding the British troops at Seringapatam heard about this image and went to see it. On entering the enclosure and on seeing the image, the impression created in his mind was such that he took off his hat and exclaimed, "O ! My God !" Further, in this connection the recent incidence of the visit of the late Prime Minister Jawaharlal Nehru, along with his daughter Smt. Indira Gandhi, the present Prime Minister of India, to Śravaṇa-Beḷagoḷa on the 7th of September 1951 only for the purpose of seeing the image of Gommaṭeśvara can be cited. On entering the enclosure when Pandit Nehru had the full view of the image, he was so much impressed by the sublime and imposing figure that he was struck with awe and wonder, continued to look at it for several minutes with concentration of mind, stood before the image in prayerful mood and ultimately exclaimed to Smt. Indira Gandhi standing nearby : "Am I standing on this earth or am I in the environment of the heaven ? I am seeing for the first time in my life such an unparalleled and pleasing image."

Moreover, a number of eminent philosophers, historians, art crtitics and archaeologists, both Indian and foreign, have expressed their expert opinions about the sublimity of the sculpture and the specific features of the image. For instance, the great western philosopher Heinrich Zimmer remarks : "It is human in shape and feature, yet as inhuman as an icicle; and thus expresses perfectly the idea of successful withdrawal from the round of life and death, personal cares, individual destiny, desires, sufferings, and events." Similarly, the well-known historian Dr. A.L. Basham, states, while referring to the colossal rock-cut medieval image of the Jaina saint Gommaṭeśvara, "He stands both upright in the posture of meditation known as 'Kāyotsarga', with feet firm on the earth, and arms held downwards but not touching the body, and he smiles faintly. The artist must have tried to express the soul almost set free from the trammels of matter, and about to leave for its final resting place of everlasting bliss at the top of the universe. Whatever the intentions of the artist, however, Gommaṭeśvara is still an ordinary young man of his time, full of calm vitality."

On the same lines, the international authority on Indian arts, Dr. Anand K. Coomaraswamy is impressed by the immoveable serenity of the image and says, "The great image of Gommateśvara is the most remarkable and one of the largest freestanding images in the world...The saint, who was the son of the first Tīrthaṅkara, and resigned his kingdom to become an ascetic, is represented in the immoveable serenity of one practising the 'kāyotsarga' austerity, undisturbed by the serpents about his feet, the anthills rising to his thighs, or the growing creeper that has already reached his shoulders."

Further, the distinguished authority on Indian architecture, Mr. Percy Brown considers this image as profoundly revealing and says, "But the earliest and most stupendous of all these great figures is the example on the Indrabeṭṭa hill depicting Gommaṭa, son of the first of the twenty-four Tīrthaṅkaras, which is a most astonishing production. This gigantic image stands over fifty-six feet high, (scarcely ten feet less than the height of the Great Sphinx in Egypt), and was carved in situ, during the reign of the Gaṅga king Rāchamalla II, to the order of his minister Chāmuṇḍa Rāya in about 983 A.D. The story of its creation is quite clear. Originally the granite antcrop forming the hill was crowned by a conspicuously lofty rock or tor, and it occurred to the imagninative mind of the Jains to fashion this solid block of gneiss into a statue of their saint. Entirely nude, as he is of the Digambara or "sky-clad" sect, and representing the ideal ascetic who stood in abstract meditation while the ant-hills arose at his feet and the creeping plants wound themselves around his limbs, this Indian colossus, in spite of defects in its proportions, is profoundly revealing. Through the surge and stress of over a thousand years this solemn and impassive figure has defied the elements, and the high finish of its workmanship still remains".

Moreover, Dr. Calambur Shivaramamurti, the most reputed art-critic and author of India, praises the sculptural skill in volved in carving out such a lofty statue and gives his opinion thus : "This huge colossus is one of the finest images of its kind in India and is a tribute to the fine workmanship of the Gaṅga sculptor."

Hence, in consideration of the unique importance of this statue of Gommaṭeśvara, it is classed as a National Monument and its protection and maintenance rests with the Department of Archaeology of the Government of India.

2. MESSAGE TO HUMANITY

From the detailed study of Śravaṇa-Beḷagoḷa it is evident that the sacred complex of Śravaṇa-Beḷagoḷa has played a dualistic part of spiritual as well as of secular importance in the history of Jainism. Its message to mankind is of great significance. It proclaims the equality and unity of all living beings on the spiritual basis and calls one and all to come near it for the adoration of Bāhubalī, the great saint of Ahiṁsā, whose colossus on the Vindhyagiri hill stands smiling and looking with half-shut eyes on the erring world. He warns the people to stop the race for material gains and to consider over the value of life. Saint Bāhubalī experienced the havoc of 'Hiṁsā', i.e., 'violence' the barbarian of an aggressor and ultimately realised the fruitlessness of the material pursuits of life. In view of this realisation, Bāhubalī renounced the world and gained eternal joy and happiness within his own Soul. It is said that even the celestial beings, who enjoy the comfort in heaven, did covet the peace and joy of Bāhubalī and came down from heaven, to worship the glorious feet of Bāhubali. But, on the other hand, the man of this world, who has listened to the message of Bāhubalī and has been a hero of both the material and spiritual realms of life, has the occasion only to rise higher and higher towards the goal of the Final.

On the whole, the history of Śravaṇa-Beḷagoḷa may be considered as the history of man's progress in life. Here the blessed spirit and scholarship of Truth and Non-violence ever guided man towards the Right Path of Emancipation. Commencing with Bhadrabāhu Swāmī, the Jaina monks of Śravaṇa-Beḷagoḷa have been the leaders of Thought and Culture. Great monks like Pūjyapāda, Prabhāchandra, Śrīdharadeva, Mallisheṇa, and many others strove to achieve distinction and devoted their precious lives to the persuit of scholarship in Grammar, Poetry, Prosody, 'Siddhānta', i.e., Philosophy, Medicine, Logic, Polity and Literature. They incessantly rendered valuable service by their sound advice and universal leadership to the people. Following their teachings kings, queens, Generals, Ministers, Merchants and even common people endeavoured to lead a life of self-control practising 'Satya and Ahiṁsā', i.e. Truth aud Non-violence. It was at the instance and advice of Siddhānta-Chakravarti Āchārya Nemichandra that the great General Chāmuṇḍa-Rāya got the blessed colossus of Bāhubalī carved and installed on the Vindhyagiri hill. Such were the men of action who, deriving inspiration from the example of Bāhubalī, devoted their time and energy in the service of humanity and sacrificed their best for the good of all. This utmost spirit of sacrifice for the welfare of the entire humanity is the central message of Śravaṇa-Beḷagoḷa.

Owing to this sublime message of self-sacrifice for the common good given by Śravaṇa-Beḷagoḷa's saints and monuments throughout its long period of history, Śravaṇa-Beḷagoḷa has ceased to be merely of sectarian interest and has become, in the real sense, a national treasure. Like the Taj Mahal of Āgrā and the Kailāśa Temple of Ellorā, the colossal image of Bāhubalī at Śravaṇa-Beḷagoḷa has attracted universal attention. It is good to bear in mind, however, that without underestimating the value of the magnificent Agra monument and the marvellous Ellorā excavation, the significane of the Jaina monuments of Śravaṇa-Beḷagoḷa is greatly deeper than the proud memories evoked by either the exquisite and the enduring fossil of a doting Emperor's dreams, or the granite efflorescence of the artistic and architectural genius of the medieval Hindus. Great as those and other antiquities undoubtedly are, the meaning of the Śravaṇa-Beḷagoḷa monuments is greater still as they enshrine the ultimate triumph of spirit over matter, show the path of Liberation based on the practice of non-violence and renunciation, and stress the values of self-sacrifice and service for the benefit of not only mankind but of all living beings.

Of course, among all the Śravaṇa-Beḷagoḷa monuments, this meaning is well represented by the gentle calm of the colossal image of Bāhubali. The basic reason for this fact is that Indian art is essentially a religious art and is considered as a mere translation into material form of the inspiration man receives from God. From this standpoint the statue of Gommaṭeśvara is a crowning achievement of Indian Art, the noblest creation of man in praise of God and a supreme embodiment of man's devotion, industry and patience. The statue impresses one tremendously with its clear-cut outline and striking pose, and it stands there defying time and weather. In this way Gommaṭeśvara stands with an expression wonderfully calm, serene and divinely radiant, looking down upon humanity as though preaching to the sinning world the basic spiritual values of non-violence, self-sacrifice and universal love—values necessary for attaining happiness in this world and beyond.

Thus we see that at Śravaṇa-Beḷagoḷa the torch of Ahiṁsā and universal love was kept burning by the Jainas during all these centuries. In this effort the image of Lord Gommaṭeśvara has been the beacon light of Jaina culture, proclaiming to the world the ideals of self-sacrifice, renunciation, tolerance, truth and Ahiṁsā, which are the milestones in the establishment of universal peace and tranquility sweeping away the clouds of war hanging over the length and breadth of the universe.

This humane message of Śravaṇa-Beḷagoḷa, the message of non-violence and universal peace, should be spread all over the world by various effective means of communication, because the world today still requires education and training in Ahiṁsā. It is absolutely necessary to bring home to the people of the world that Ahiṁsā or non-violence is not merely a theoretical principle but also a practical way of life which can solve various problems clamouring for solution in the world and can thus help in establishing universal peace and goodwill among the nations. For realising this purpose International Institutes for studies in Ahiṁsā and in Comparative Religion will have to be started. Obviously, Śravaṇa-Beḷagoḷa is an ideal sacred place for carrying on this work on international scale, as it has got the noble tradition of doing this kind of work continuously for the last several centuries. Śravaṇa-Beḷagoḷa is destined to play this in the international field in the years to come and it has already started the work in this direction under the spiritual guidance of the Preceptor of World Religion and the Great Saint of India, Elāchārya Munishree Vidyānand Mahārāj. It is hoped that Śravaṇa-Beḷagoḷa', will soon become the 'Viśva-Tīrtha' "The World's Sacred Place".

BIBLIOGRAPHY

(A) BOOKS IN ENGLISH

Basham, A.L. : The Wonder That Was India. (Sidgwick & Jackson, London, 1954).

Brown, Percy : Indian Architecture (Buddhist and Hindu) (Taraporevala, Bombay, 1965).

Coomaraswamy, A.K. : History of Indian and Indonesian Art (Dover Publications, New York, 1965).

Derrett, J.D.M. : The Hoysalas : A Medieval Indian Royal Family. (Oxford Univ. Press. Madras. 1957).

Desai, P.B. : Jainism in South India and Some Jaina Epigraphs. (Jain Sanskriti Samrakshak Sangha, Solapur, 1957).

Fergusson, James : History of Indian and Eastern Architecture, Vols. I & II. (John Murray. London, 1910).

Fiseher, Klaus : Caves and Temples of the Jains. (World Jain Mission, Aliganj, 1957).

Ghosh, A. (Ed.) : Jaina Arts and Architecture, Vols. I to III (Bharatiya Jnanapith, New Delhi, 1974).

Jain, Jyoti Prasad : The Jaina Sources of the History of Ancient India. (Munshi Ram, Delhi, 1964).

Jain, Kamta Prasad : The Religion of Tirthankaras (World Jain Mission, Aliganj, 1964).

Jindal, K.B. : The Prefaces (Jindal, Calcutta, 1958).

Mahāmastakābhisheka : Souvenir, 1953. (Poornima Publications, Bangalore, 1953).

Majumdar, R.C. (Ed.) : The History and Culture of the Indian People, Vol. II. (Bharatiya Vidya Bhavan, Bombay, 1951).

Mallinath, C.S. : Glory of Gommateshvara. (Mercury Publishing, Madras, 1953).

Mookarji, Radha Kumud : Ancient India (Indian Press, Allahabad, 1956).

-do- : Chandragupta Maurya and His Times. (Motilal Banarasidas, Delhi, 1966).

Murty, H.V.S. and Ramkrishnan, R : A History of Karnataka (S. Chand, New Delhi, 1978).

Narasimhachar, R. : Epigraphia Carnatica, Vol. II, Inscriptions at Shravana-Belagola. (Mysore Govt. Press, Bangalore, 1923).

Ramchandran, T.N. : Jaina Monuments of India (Vira Shasana Sangh, Calcutta, 1944).

Ramchandra Rao, S.K. : Jainism in South India (Oriental Research Trust, Madras, 1970).

Report on the Working of the : Mahamastakabhisheka Ceremony of Shri Gommateshvar Svamy at Sravanabelagola held on 5th March, 1953. (Govt. Press, Bangalore, 1961).

Rice, Lewis, B. : Inscriptions at Shravana Belagola (Archaeological Deptt., Mysore, 1889).

-do- : Mysore and Coorg from the Inscriptions (Archibald Constable, London, 1909).

Saletore, B.A. : Medieval Jainism (Karnatak Publishing House, Bombay, 1938).

Sangave, V.A. : Jaina Community—A Social Survey (Second Edition) (Popular Prakashan, Bombay, 1980).

Sastri, K.A. Nilakanta (Ed.) : Age of the Nandas and Mauryas (Motilal Banarasidas, Banaras, 1952).

Shah, U.P. and Dhaky, M.A. (Ed.) : Aspects of Jaina Art and Architecture. (Gujarat Government, Ahmedabad, 1975).

Sharma, S.R. : Jainism and Karnataka Culture (Karnatka Historical Research Society, Dharwar, 1940).

Sivaramamurti, C. : Indian Sculpture (Allied Publishers, Bombay, 1961).

-do- : The Art of India (H.N. Abrams, New York, 1977).

Smith, Vincent, A. : History of India, (Oxford Univ., 1923).

-do- : The Early History of India, (Fourth Edition) (Oxford Univ., 1957).

Theodore de Bary (Ed.) : Sources of Indian Tradition (Columbia Univ., New York, 1958).

Workman, W.H. : Through Town and Jungle (London, 1904).

(B) BOOKS IN HINDI

Divakara, S.C. : Vishvatīrtha Śramanavelagola (All India Dig. Jain Tirthakshetra Committee, Bombay, 1967).

Jain, Hira Lal : Jaina Śilālekha Saṅgraha. (Manikchand Dig. Jain Granthamala, Bombay, 1928).

Jain, Jyoti Prasad : Pramukha Aitihāsik Jaina Purusha aura Mahilāyen. (Bharatiya Jnanapith, New Delhi, 1975).

Jain, Lakmi Chandra : Antardvandon ke Pāra : Gommateshvara Bāhubali (Bharatiya Jnanapith. New Delhi, 1979).

Jain, Raja Krishna : Śravanabeḷagoḷa Aur Dakshina-ke Anya Jaina Tirth (Viraseva Mandir, Delhi, 1953).

Jain, Surendra Nath : Jaina Badri-ke Bāhubalī Tathā Dakshina-ke Anya Jaina Tīrtha. (Jain Publicity Bureau, Bombay, 1953).

(C) JOURNALS

Indian Antiquary
Jaina Antiquary
Jaina Gazette
Voice of Ahimsa
Jaina Siddhanta Bhaskara (Hindi)
Sanmati (Marathi)

BY THE SAME AUTHOR

* **Jaina Community—A Social Survey**
  (*S cond Edition, 1980*)
* **Life and Legacy of Mahavira—A Social Study**
  (*First Edition, 1975*)
* **History of Dakshina Bharat Jaina Sabha**
  (*First Edition, 1976*)
* **Story of Mahavira**
  (*First Edition, 1963*)
* **Outlines of Jainism**
  (*Revised Edition, 1975*)
* **Sociology**
  (*Third Edition, 1972*)
* **Sociology** (Kannada Translation)
  (*First Edition, 1971*)
* **Social Anthropology** (in Marathi)
  (*Second Edition, 1976*)
* **Social Anthropology** (Gujarati Translation)
  (*First Edition, 1971*)
* **Primitive Social Life** (in Marathi)
  (*Second Edition, 1978*)
* **Introduction to Sociology** (in Marathi)
  (*Second Edition, 1975*)
* **Social Problems in India** (in Marathi)
  (*First Edition, 1979*)
* **Elacharya Munishree Vidyanand** (in Marathi)
  (*First Edition, 1980*)